Advance Pra .... _ty_

"Dharma can be lightened and sweetened till it goes down like elevator music. It can thrash and wail like punk. Here, it's like Bach—not whispering, not shouting, but unfolding from within itself, with the steady, implacable rhythms of elemental truth in the act of discovering itself. Genoud drills deep. This is not a solemn book but it's a serious one. You can't whip through it like a spiritual beach novel. Read each paragraph or stanza slowly and contemplatively (and, when necessary, repeatedly). Most of all, bring its insights into your practice and your life."

—Dean Sluyter, author of *Fear Less* and *Natural Meditation*

"Charles Genoud doesn't just explain Buddhist principles of awakening, but evokes awakened awareness out of his readers. His words pull us out of the frameworks we have mistaken for reality and draw us into deepening intimacy with the nature of experience where inmost freedom is found. Genoud speaks directly from the naked awareness to which he points, giving tremendous immediacy and freshness to every sentence of this amazing work."

—John Makransky, author of *Awakening through Love*

"*Beyond Tranquility* is a precious and insightful reflection on bondage and freedom. This book deserves wide readership."

—Christopher Titmuss, cofounder of Gaia House
and author of *Buddhist Wisdom for Daily Living*

BEYOND TRANQUILITY

Buddhist Meditations in Essay and Verse

By Charles Genoud

*Translated from the French
by Anna Iatseko and Charles Genoud*

Wisdom Publications
199 Elm Street
Somerville, MA 02144 USA
wisdomexperience.org

Library of Congress Cataloging-in-Publication Data
Names: Genoud, Charles, author. | Iatseko, Anna, translator.
Title: Beyond tranquility: Buddhist meditations in essay and verse / by Charles
    Genoud; translated from the French by Anna Iatseko and Charles Genoud.
Description: Somerville: Wisdom Publications, 2020. | Description based on print
    version record and CIP data provided by publisher; resource not viewed.
Identifiers: LCCN 2019025438 (print) | LCCN 2019025439 (ebook) |
    ISBN 9781614296058 (ebook) | ISBN 9781614295815 (paperback) |
    ISBN 9781614295815 (paperback) | ISBN 9781614296058 (ebook)
Subjects: LCSH: Peace—Religious aspects—Buddhism.
Classification: LCC BQ4570.P4 (ebook) | LCC BQ4570.P4 G4613 2020 (print) |
    DDC 294.3/4432—dc23
LC record available at https://lccn.loc.gov/2019025438

ISBN 978-1-61429-581-5   ebook ISBN 978-1-61429-605-8

24 23 22 21 20
5   4   3   2   1

Cover design by Marc Whitaker. Interior design by Tony Lulek.

Printed on acid-free paper that meets the guidelines for permanence and durability of
the Production Guidelines for Book Longevity of the Council on Library Resources.

Printed in the United States of America.

Please visit fscus.org.

Contents

PART TWO: REFLECTIONS IN ESSAY

introduction

BUDDHISM EXISTS FOR ONLY ONE PURPOSE: to illuminate the human condition, its fragility and its freedom. Like a raft used to cross a river, Buddhism is a means, not an end. To make it into an object of veneration turns the means into a burden.

Although it is sometimes wise to challenge tradition, it is also important to let oneself be challenged by it. Then, to embark on the Buddha's paths as a means of exploring human nature can lead to surprising discoveries.

Many contemporary books describe the techniques and countless benefits of meditation; few attempt to unveil it. The task is not easy because meditation lies in the heart of human experience, before language speaks for it. This attempt at unveiling will, inevitably, fail. Language casts a shadow on whatever it attempts to grasp. Nevertheless, it is through language that it is possible, finally, to leave off language's grasping.

Meditation cannot be reduced to an insatiable quest for happiness. It must be left to itself.

What is at stake in meditation is timeless. It cannot merely serve the purpose of a particular era without limiting itself to the profane and the mundane. But in every era, the language that expresses it must be revisited.

Learning, reflection, and meditation are the three sources of knowledge for the Buddhist tradition. They are all used to explore ever deeper within oneself.

Learning—the first source—is knowledge that comes from others.

The second source—reflection—attempts a coherent reorganization of what has been learned, retaining certain notions and rejecting others. This requires correct understanding of the teachings as well as deep intimacy with one's own thinking process.

Thought plays an important role because in daily life one must think, plan, and make decisions. The clearer thinking is, the wiser the decisions will be.

A great part of Buddhist literature is devoted to substantiating this kind of thinking. The Tibetan tradition, which is particularly rich in this area, offers numerous spiritual exercises organized in a very skillful, intellectually rigorous way.

These two sources of knowledge are based on concepts and, therefore, on an interpretation of experiences.

Finally, meditation—the last of the three elements—frees itself from reason. It lies beyond concepts, beliefs, and dogmas.

> Having abandoned what is taken up, not clinging,
> one does not create a dependency even on knowledge.
> Not taking sides among those who are divided,
> one does not fall back on any view at all. (Paramatthaka Sutta)

In the Buddhist tradition, the deep meditative experience, not the doctrinal texts, is the ultimate authority.

This point of view is shared by the contemporary writer Maurice Blanchot:

> One must also return to the mystics [meditators]: the only ones, among all the philosophers, who openly test and in the end realize their philosophy, but especially because it is no longer a matter, in this movement, of knowing but of being.

But this inner experience must be pursued with discipline in order to ensure that it goes beyond what is merly personal and imaginary. Rather than using sophisticated techniques, this discipline lies in the suspension of all activity, all technique. Only then can meditation lead to an independence of mind that allows one not only to think for oneself, but, what is more important, to disengage utterly from the grip of thought. Finally, the meditator must return to the world of ideas and action, motivated by thoughts enlightened by her inner experience.

What the inner experience unveils needs to be integrated into daily life by concepts.

There are differences within Buddhism, so any perspective will always be partial. This book is, of course, no exception. There are, however, common notions shared by all Buddhists.

- All components are impermanent.
- A life of confusion always leaves desires unfulfilled.
- There is nothing independent and immutable in the human being that can be called "I."
- It is possible to free oneself from confusion and dissatisfaction once and for all.

This book never departs from this Buddhist vision of the world—at least not deliberately.

A point of view commonly shared by Buddhist masters that is particularly significant here states that the spiritual path, and meditation specifically, consists essentially of nongrasping.

Sakya Pandita, a thirteenth-century Tibetan Buddhist master, taught: "If there is grasping, there is no wisdom." In the twentieth century, the Burmese master Mahasi Sayadaw taught that we meditate in order to not grasp, in perfect agreement with the Buddha's words that "The absence of grasping is freedom."

The meditations described in this book are based on the Theravada Buddhist tradition, mainly as taught in Burma, and on the Tibetan tradition, with a few remarks taken from Zen. These approaches complement each other. Vipassana, a characteristic Theravada practice following the Satipatthana Sutta, is very careful to include in meditation all aspects of life, such as the body, feelings, thoughts, emotions, and mental states, negative as well as positive.

The Tibetan tradition analyzes thoughts and emotions in great depth, to discover the elusive nature of consciousness and of the world. Zen approaches meditation in a comprehensive manner as it integrates simple movements and daily activities.

Because empathy must supplement wisdom in order to ensure responsible behavior in the world, a meditation on kindness also appears in this book.

The texts most frequently cited to describe meditation are early Sutras: the Satipatthana Sutta, the Bahia Sutta, the Malunkyaputta Sutta, the Sivaka Sutta, and the Kaccayanagotta Sutta. For the meditations on thoughts and emotions, passages from early Tibetan texts are used, as well as the oral teachings of the great twentieth-century Tibetan master Dilgo Khyentse Rinpoche.

In general, the philosophical point of view expressed here is consistent with the texts of the great Indian Buddhist philosopher Nagarjuna as well as with the Vimalakirti Sutra, one of the main sutras that expounds the "middle way," the Madhyamaka philosophy.

Teachers from other spiritual traditions are also cited here, including Saint Augustine, Meister Eckhart, and Martin Buber. They shed light on certain important aspects of the spiritual path and are a great source of inspiration.

Any system of thought is eventually caught in its own game. The study of other systems may help to avoid that fate, at least partially. The reification of the Buddha nature by certain authors—the erroneous interpretation of it as a kind of "thing" to be grasped—can serve as an example. Meister Eckhart specifically underlines the danger of grasping at the ultimate when he teaches that we must pray to God to free us of God.

The reflections presented in the second part of this book draw on even more varied sources.

The chapter in that section on the investigation of consciousness was enhanced by the readings of Jean-Paul Sartre's early texts, such as *The Imaginary: A Phenomenological Psychology of the Imagination* and *The Transcendence of the Ego*. The works of Friedrich Nietzsche, Simone Weil, Martin Buber, and Sartre have deeply influenced the outlook on morality expressed here.

Meditations are presented immediately after this introduction so they may be approached with a certain degree of innocence. The reflections come last and attempt to support what might otherwise seem dogmatic in the material dealing with meditation.

Each chapter of this book has been designed to function on its own. This has required a certain amount of repetition, so as not to impose a sequential reading order.

There are already numerous books expounding Buddhist doctrine. This one is, rather, an invitation to inner experience.

PART ONE

Meditations in Verse

the past never was

these simple words
give rise to a strange feeling

the phrase is almost insignificant
it could go unnoticed

but when we stop to consider it

the past never was?

Joseph Campbell describes
the traditional itinerary of a hero or a shaman
his birth, miraculous, a sign of an exceptional destiny
he forgets it and merges into the familiar world
until the day when an event reminds him of his destiny

an event seemingly trivial
a slight disturbance in the order of the world
a thing not quite in its place

a cup that shatters
startling words
an incomprehensible sickness

an ordinary person would pass by
without noticing this breach
in the reality of the everyday
but the shaman is profoundly unsettled

she is compelled to engage with this opening
and will not rest before discovering
a new vision of the world
a greater vision
one that comprehends the incomprehensible

the past never was
I never found the source of this quotation
did I read it in a text by Maurice Blanchot?

I keep on churning these few words in my mind

what do they mean?

temporality troubled the greatest of the Christian theologians
if no one asks me what time is, I know
if I am asked, I know no more
God help me, Saint Augustine confesses

he did not escape his destiny, thank God

the past never was sounds like a koan
these apparently trivial words
possess a similar challenging power

according to Buddhism
human beings are prisoners not of reality
but of their beliefs

meditation is liberating insofar as it challenges
the validity of these beliefs

to think that it is possible to
engage in meditation without being willing
to be unsettled by its challenging nature
is absurd

like wanting to step into the cool waters of a river without getting wet

desacralization

desacralization of meditation renders it futile
like cocktail party chatter

the sacred, atemporal, cannot serve a purpose
it cannot be reduced to something useful
on the contrary

rooted in a culture, religion is situated in time
it has a history, a dogma, beliefs
beliefs rightly challenged by science

it is, however, also the guardian of the sacred
of the inconceivable
about which science has no say
a fact hardly acknowledged

Meister Eckhart calls them merchants of the temple
these devotees who praise God
to have their wishes granted
asking God for favors in exchange for their praise
they are in the temple, but remain profane

to reduce meditation to a technique for well-being
to confine it to the useful and the profitable
is to desacralize it

the temple, in meditation
is the experience of the meditator
we need to surrender to it
not to contemplate it from a distance
not to observe the breathing, the sensations, the emotions
but to be each experience

when the meditator is willing to get in the game
each position, each movement of the body is a sacred place
where existence reveals itself, in its entirety

the Satipatthana Sutta expresses it simply
when the meditator is walking, she is aware
when turning the head, when bending or stretching the arm
she is aware

thus, in all positions, all activities
even the most ordinary ones
it is about being, not about doing

Martha Graham said the movement never lies
the secret it reveals is that of a body of presence
that is not reduced to a means of carrying out tasks

this does not mean that the meditator forbids herself
all activity
that she confines herself to a vain passivity
but that within the action
she does not lose herself in the objective to be reached

having become indifferent to the fruits of the actions
always fulfilled
dependent on nothing
he does not act
as busy as he may seem
—the Bhagavad-Gita

according to Mircea Eliade
the sacred is the place of the most dense presence
the living body is, thus, a sanctuary

to be sitting, is to be awakened
according to Zen Master Dogen

all activities—eating, drinking, sweeping the garden path—
are the places of meditation and of awakening

awareness / knowingness

without distinguishing awareness from knowledge
without distinguishing being aware from knowing
it is impossible to understand what is meditation

from a very young age a child learns
to know the surrounding world
to distinguish what is dangerous from what is not
to name things

university education and professional training
are also an accumulation of knowledge
not only about things
but also methods, techniques

knowledge transposes every experience into data
that can be kept in memory
concepts and names are the means of this transposition

as soon as an experience arises
a perception of a sound of a shape
it is interpreted

ah! I hear the neighbor starting his car
while, in fact, I only hear a roar
we always hear more than what we hear

I walk into my office, I move around
at any given moment what I see is totally different
and yet, I believe that I am seeing the same thing:
the office

this unchanging office is but a concept
kept in memory

there is a difference between
seeing colors in the sky at sunrise
and remembering these colors

when a concept is substituted for an experience
confusion arises between what is seen and what is thought

any interpretations made by knowledge can be false
maybe it's not my neighbor's car that I hear
but it is indisputable that I hear

in knowledge, a unique experience is abandoned
for a general idea
the word fixes the event
and renders it objective and universal

by its nature, the concept implies duration
even if it does not explicitly express any notions of time

the name sunset
can be applied from the first instant
to the last of the event
when the sun is about to disappear
yet the name does not change

subjected to the primacy of knowledge
we are exiled in thought, in the abstract

knowledge is limited to what is general
but its occurrence also reveals awareness
the theatre of this exile

an awareness that cannot be reduced to knowledge

if we were not conscious of knowing
knowing would not be different from not knowing
to know is to know that one knows, or, more precisely
to know is to be aware of knowing

in any experience, consciousness is also self-consciousness
when it hears a bird singing
it is aware of hearing

this consciousness of hearing requires no concept
it is not a knowledge
it cannot be grasped, kept
it cannot be mistaken

to evoke this self-consciousness
the word *presence* is used
and sometimes *mindfulness* or *awareness*

every conscious existence exists
as consciousness of existing
—Sartre

this self-consciousness is not an activity
it does not require any particular intention
for consciousness, to be is to be conscious

the flame of a candle just shines
it makes no sense to say it lights itself

in any given experience
it is possible not to cling to knowledge
and thus allow the unveiling of awareness

the point is not to make oneself empty
but to let go of one-sided interest in the known
and let awareness be unveiled

to hear
and not to look for the source of the sound

not to hang onto the notion of car
so the consciousness of hearing can unveil itself

meditation

meditation is not an activity, a technique
it is a way of being
a way that can be present in everything we do

an activity tends toward a goal
necessarily imaginary
since it is yet to come

constantly having an objective in focus
the mind absorbs itself into the virtual
it cuts itself from reality

but meditation is about reality

just as the dancer is the dance
the meditator is the meditation

when the practice of meditation is understood
as a means of accomplishing something
it transforms the one who meditates into a tool

when a man plows his field
he becomes a plowman
the field to be plowed becomes what matters
not the one who plows

absorbed in his work
the plowman becomes the tool through which
the work is done
he gains a harvest
but loses the being he is

a tool is nothing in itself
it only exists so that the work can be done
a branch to saw, a board to be planed

the hammer is nothing without the nail
it exists only for the future
its presence is blurred like a photo
of a moving object

the meditator, busy transforming himself
calming agitation
eliminating drowsiness
and pain is made into a tool

he may gain calm
but he loses his being

during practice
the question repeatedly arises
what to do?
yet meditation is not a question of doing
but of suspending all aims
all intent

if a question must surface
it should rather be
where is my presence in this instant?

meditating means being open
to the present experience
but this experience is always already here
there is nothing to do
simply to be

to go to sleep
we avoid stimulation
the light and the noise
we lie down and let go of the intention
of doing anything
even the intention of sleeping

there is nothing to do in meditation
but isn't that what most people do in daily life
not caring to be present

and so remaining
at the surface of things

there is nothing to do to be present
but stop wanting things to be different
and surrender to the present experience

meditation is not a specific activity
but a state of presence in each moment
in activity as well as in idleness

according to Beckett, Joyce's writing is not
about something, it is that very thing

meditation is not about something
it is the thing itself
neither useful nor useless

it is a reversal of interest
that finally relies on the being of the doer

in the museum
Marcel Duchamp's puzzling sculpture
a bottle rack
standing for itself
not for the bottles

the present

the present has no history
neither brief nor eternal
without before or after
it is not situated in time

wanting to locate it between past and future
is to insert it into temporality
into a tale

to transpose the elusive real
into a story—even a very brief one—
that can be reduced to a single word
a story one can remember
is to live one's present life
as if it were a memory

a present between past and future
drawn to the known by a word
already belongs to the past

it has fallen into the order of things
it has become lifeless

a felt experience left to itself
has no certitude nor incertitude
it is free

but the meditator
becomes attached to certain experiences
to calm, serenity, alertness
at the expense of self-awareness

thus he constantly endeavors
to transform his experience
to eliminate agitation, sleepiness, difficulties
to seek clarity and joy

it takes time to transform
as short as it may be

wanting this, not wanting that
we enter into a story and its limits

stoic exhortation to not want things to happen
as we want them to happen
but to want them to happen as they happen
does not lead to resignation
it removes the experience from the narrative
from any evaluation

for the meditator it is a matter of openness
to every experience
without imposing a form on it
without judging it
resignation is a verdict
a figment of experience

perhaps, aware of this danger
Nietzsche points out
that we should not simply want things
to happen as they happen
but should love the way they happen

the nuance Nietzsche brings
applied to meditation
sometimes helps to bridge this distance
from the experience
that resignation and patience still imply

the meditator may believe
she is feeling a difficult experience
without reluctance
but when she gives herself to love it
she is surprised by a release
by a greater availability
which results from the union
of the meditator's being and her experience

to love life is to open to it
unconditionally

then the being of this emotion or that sensation
can be revealed
without concepts

freed from all notions
the felt experience is self-awareness

an experience without grasping
gives the measure
of what freedom or nirvana could be

the present is without a story, without anyone
but it is not lifeless

suffering

the Buddha is not a prophet
or a pundit
he is not of divine essence

simply a man looking at the human condition
without complacency

a man facing disease, old age, and death
and separation
facing mourning, failures, successes
joys, and pains

is suffering inherent
to the human condition?

in his meditation,
the Buddha repeatedly comes back
to this question
and he does not want hasty conclusions or
to look for answers in the hereafter

he is not pessimistic,
but extraordinarily ambitious

if there is a meaning to human suffering
it can only be found within oneself

some people look for a spiritual path
as a means of escape
they want to escape from themselves

they are attracted by an ideal of perfection
which mirrors back a glorified image of themselves

they only long for what is beautiful, high, and luminous
and reject what is low, dark, and vulgar

although understandable
this motivation only exacerbates frustration

speaking of fulfillment, Simone Weil remarks
what people are looking for is not wrong
but they are looking for it in the wrong place

Buddhism asserts we can exceed the limits
of the human condition
by freeing ourselves from confusion

to think that a human being is contingent upon a past
that one is a victim of it
removes the possibility of freeing oneself from it

as long as a person plays the victim
one is not the master of one's destiny
the key to his freedom is in the hands
of the perpetrator
or in what constrains him

we cannot return to the past
to undo it

we are quick to use the notion of karma
to justify a difficult situation

on this subject
the sutra of two arrows sheds a wise and subtle light

in this sermon the Buddha affirms
that ordinary beings
like the wise disciples
also experience painful sensations
so, what difference does it make being awakened or not

when an ordinary being feels pain
he laments, he complains
he identifies with the pain
he turns to pleasures because he has no other solution
it is as if having received a first arrow
he receives a second one, where the first wound is

when a wise disciple feels pain
she does not lament, she does not complain
she does not turn to sensual pleasures
because she knows another solution
she does not identify with the pain
she knows its true nature

it shows that what torments the ordinary being
is not his past, but his attitude toward the present

what torments us
is not our past
but the present situation
distorted by the presence of past memories

yet human existence would be shallow and dull
if everything were just a reaction to the present situation

at the beginning of the analysis
of the chain of conditioning
Buddhism inserts a link it calls *samskara*
to account for the traces of the past experiences
affecting the present situation
this gives a clear psychological dimension
to the notion of karma

humans' difficulties are not only problems
of disease, old age, and death
today we must talk of depression, meaninglessness
and disconnection from reality

meditation is not recommended in all cases
to practice it requires a certain capacity
for self-consciousness

that this self-consciousness is not accompanied
by deep anxieties
or abysmal sadness

meditation is not a substitute for psychotherapy
even though it shares some of its benefits

in meditation, imprints of past experiences sometimes emerge
a forgotten sadness, an incomprehensible worry
images of ancient trauma

this is because the meditator is welcoming
all emergent experiences
without judgment
without control

there is also a therapeutic dimension to meditation
how to expect spiritual freedom
when one is still bound by psychological disorders

it is not simply a question of recognizing, of naming them
which pertains to knowledge
but to be aware of them

to live an experience without identifying with it
to leave it in an impersonal and atemporal way
is particular to vipassana, to dzogchen, and to zazen

it is about letting emerge into consciousness
that which moves us without our knowing it

how could there be freedom
without knowing that we are moved by certain drives?

when the practitioner's mind is troubled by desire
he is aware that his mind is troubled by desire
that is what the sutra on mindfulness recommends
it adds nothing

thus, the distinction
between knowing and being aware
is essential

practicing vipassana means being present
moment by moment
free from confusion

being present is a way of distinguishing
the real from the imaginary

the Satipatthana Sutta lists
the different aspects of the practice

first, to calm the mind, the attention is focused on breathing
is it short or long
superficial or deep?

it is sometimes recommended to count breaths
up to 7 or 21 and start again

the Buddha did not seek salvation in texts
but in the daily life
in the most ordinary
in the living body

throughout the day
the meditator is present in her body
whether lying down
sitting, standing, or in movement

to jump endlessly from one experience to another
without fully experiencing any
makes it impossible to know what they really are

to calm her mind
the meditator avoids losing herself in agitation
when a thought or an image arises
she does not hold onto it
she focuses on breathing again

little by little, the mind settles
it becomes sharper, more penetrating

but this sutra does not concern the development of tranquility
but rather that of wisdom

the point is not to fix the mind on a chosen phenomenon
but to be aware of any experience
a way of being called *sati* in the text

in a systematic way, experiences are grouped
into four domains
the body, feeling tones, thoughts, and emotions
and finally, mental states such as calm, concentration,
sleepiness, and agitation

these include all experiences of life

meditation is not a specific experience
but the relation to the experience

whether there is calm or agitation, sadness or joy
the point is to not cling to it or resist it
but to open to it
and to experience it thoroughly

the attention paid to the body
is described in a simple way
when a meditator is standing
she is aware of being standing
when she is sitting
she is aware of being sitting

when she stretches or bends an arm
when she turns her head
when she looks down or straight ahead

she is aware when she eats
when she drinks, when she lies down
she is present in all activities

in a more formal way, in a sitting meditation
she is present to bodily sensations
without confusing the image of the body
with the sensations

a bodily sensation has no shape, no color
it is a perception of heaviness or lightness
a certain feeling of warmth or of freshness

the sensation is not to be observed
which would imply a distancing from it
but to be felt

the sensation should not be confused with an object
a confusion noted by Condillac:

philosophy makes a step forward: it discovers that sensations are not the
qualities of objects, but, on the contrary, that they are a modification
of the soul

in formal practice
it is recommended to begin by choosing an anchor
like the sensations in the abdomen or in the chest
to try to feel the sensations there
without naming each experience

when the mind loses itself in memory or in anticipation
one must simply become aware of it
and focus on the anchor

in this way, little by little
the sensation can be experienced
with great sensitivity

when a pain is felt, the meditator tends to focus
on the concept *pain*
instead of being interested in the experience itself
the concept makes it difficult to feel the sensation intimately

when the meditator does not stop at the concept *pain*
"pain" may disappear
there remains only a sharp sensation
which is no longer experienced as being unbearable

hearing can be a useful point of anchorage
for some people

usually, when we hear a sound
we want to know what it reveals
a bird on a branch, a door being opened
the sound itself is of little interest to us

the Italian futurist Luigi Russolo had a passion for noises
wherever we are, what we hear is always noise
if we ignore it, it disturbs us
if we pay attention to it, it becomes fascinating

then, when a sound is heard
we are not concerned by what it reveals
but we are aware of hearing the sound

enjoying the richness of the hearing experience
the meditator is simply hearing

when we listen or when we watch
we tend to step out of ourselves
to project ourselves toward the source of the sound
or into the space we are looking at

meditation is about letting perceptions arise
not stepping out of ourselves
then perception is neither inside nor outside
it is the totality of my being at that moment

it is similar for all sensory experiences
to be not only aware of color, but aware of seeing

this awareness of seeing, hearing
feeling a bodily sensation
is self-awareness
it is presence

when the mind is more settled
we can be present in each experience
each bodily sensation
each emotion or mental state
such as fatigue or tranquility

then we need not come back to the anchor

experience is not just pure perception
it touches us emotionally
it may suit us or not
we seek it or we reject it
sometimes we are just indifferent

the affective dimension
constitutes the second aspect of experience
to be included in meditation

even though we may not be aware of it
each experience is felt as pleasant
unpleasant or neutral

we unconsciously react
to this aspect of the experience
through attachment
rejection
or indifference

these reactions
reveal a confused relationship to our experience
meditative practice aims at dissipating this confusion
this is what the term *vipassana* means
to see clearly beyond all misapprehension

this feeling tone of pleasant, unpleasant
or neutral
is the value that mostly unconsciously
governs our life

we are constantly seeking pleasures
no matter how small

be they simple
like eating a piece of cake
drinking a cup of tea
or more sophisticated
like listening to music
it is always a search for pleasure

we are affected by the slightest discomfort
when a discomfort arises
we react immediately
to reduce it or to eliminate it

we adhere to these value criteria
without even realizing it

for the pleasure criterion
Buddhism substitutes that of freedom
something upheld also by some Greek philosophers

when we pay attention
to the unpleasant aspect
of an experience
we realize that we are not forced to avoid it
it is unpleasant, and so what?

during practice
experiences of calm and serenity can arise
it is necessary to let go of attachment
to the sometimes extremely pleasant aspects
of these experiences

without denying the pleasure, just the dependency on it
to be free from the hold of the feeling tones

in winter, the sky is often luminous
on the East Coast of the United States

one day, as I was contemplating the sunset
I realized how pleasant this experience was

relinquishing attachment
there remained for me only the seeing
of the sky colors
and a feeling of freedom

then the fading of the sunset
did not produce a feeling of loss

an indifferent experience
generates only a lack of interest
the mind does not fully engage with it

being aware of a neutral feeling tone
allows us to substitute
curiosity for lack of interest
insight for confusion

difficulties

in cases of particularly difficult experiences
the simple intention of being present
is not the most skillful means

meditation, in the sense that we understand it here
calls for an open and receptive attitude
it does not take on any particular task
such as focusing the mind on breathing

this allows for traces of repressed experience
to resurface at the conscious level

some very painful truths
sometimes linked to early childhood
can resurface in the mind

it then becomes important to introduce strategies
so as not to generate more pain and confusion
and not to exacerbate the trauma

intense emotions
affect the body in obvious ways
heaviness on the chest, difficult breathing
abdominal pain, for example

in meditation, it is recommended
to choose a zone of attention
that is larger than the painful area
to include shoulders and arms too, for example

in this way, the meditator can avoid being absorbed
in the difficult area
it creates a space that is more alive

it is sometimes recommended to link the practice of lovingkindness
to that of vipassana

when we are angry or sad
we may unconsciously hold our breath
then we try to correct the way we breathe
only adding a constraint to a constraint

it is better to notice how breathing is inhibited
which parts of the body are being held rigidly
to avoid feeling

this requires sensitivity
thus the meditator can gradually become more aware
and, perhaps
understand the reason behind this inhibition
could it be an emotion held in the chest?

being willing, little by little, to feel the emotion
its meaning may unveil itself
the need to block the ribcage may disappear
and breathing flow freely

during intense meditation retreats
it is sometimes wise to ease up on the practice
to go for a walk, to listen to nature

meditation and psychotherapy share certain features
for example, they both allow unconscious contents
to resurface into consciousness

psychotherapy is sometimes better adapted
to certain problems

but let's come back to meditation
by repeatedly returning to the anchor
the mind can be stabilized
and acquire the ability to stay open and receptive

not as a means of avoiding difficult emotions
but as a deepening of the contact with reality

absence

the word *presence* expresses well the meditative attitude

this attitude is not easy to develop
beginners quickly discover how absent they are
even if that is not their intention

often meditators try to remediate absence
by focusing on a sensation or the breath
as if presence had some specific location

but we may also seek to find out
where we are when absent

this capacity of the mind
to veil itself is an amazing thing—
how can it accomplish this magic trick?

the word *presence* evokes the notion
of temporality
the present is defined in relation
to the past and the future

is to be lost in the past or the future
an obstacle to presence?

we are experts at being lost in memories
or absorbed in anticipation
how many times do we run the scenario of what could happen?

Mark Twain is supposed to have said
the worst events in my life never happened

but we can also get lost in the future
in a more subtle way
by wanting to transform or improve
what is being experienced

the image of the enhanced
experience becomes a substitute
for the experience itself
thus we slip into fantasy
but this image is modeled on the appearance
of the present experience
only slightly modified
so the trick goes unnoticed

wanting to transform what happens during meditation
is an efficient way to be absent

the present is nothing but an instance
of temporality
situated between past and future
it is not more real

to name each experience present, is useless

when one is absorbed in listening to a sound
there is no concept of present or now

a sensation experienced in the abdomen
in the chest or the knee
is out of temporality

the Dhammapada says simply
let go of the past
let go of the future
let go of the present

presence is also the opposite of absence
absence means being out of, far from
out of what?
out of oneself

to be lost in a discussion
to be absorbed in a game of chess

a pool player can be taken by the game
aware of the trajectory of the ball he has just hit
he is not distracted, and yet he is not present
he is concentrated

it is not simply about being aware
of a bird singing
on a branch
one needs to be aware of hearing
of seeing, of tasting

when we are absent
it does not mean that we have suddenly disappeared
we are still here
but we are absorbed in the content of the experience
lost in the bird singing, absorbed in thought

the location of presence and of absence is the same

when I get lost in the past
it is still a present experience
I cannot go into the past

to be lost in an accounting problem
or in memories
are similar ways of being absorbed
in the content of the experience

just as when we are captivated
by the colors of the sunset

the problem is not with the image
of the past or of the future
they are just content, like any other
the problem is being absorbed into the content

memory can only arise in the present

at every moment there is an awareness
of something
when too much importance is given
to the thing perceived
or thought of
self-awareness weakens

the place of absence
is the content of perception or thought
that of presence is the consciousness of being aware
of something
the consciousness of seeing, not of what is seen
the consciousness of thinking, not of what is thought
they are the same experience

consciousness is absent
or at least seems to go absent
when it takes itself to be what it is conscious of
like a window that takes itself for the form it reflects

one of the most commonly reflected forms is that of the *I*
we must realize its imaginary nature

but consciousness and content coincide perfectly
the reflection cannot be separated from the glass

to believe that that presence is experienced in tranquility
in the absence of thought, in serenity
is to situate it wrongly

presence is not an experience
it is a way of being in the experience
it is an attitude, not an objective

thoughts

thoughts are not an obstacle to meditation
as many people imagine

as early as the eleventh century
the Tibetan Master Gampopa remarked
nowadays people don't know how to meditate
they want to eliminate thoughts

thoughts dominate our existence
without them, there would be nothing
no babies, no wars, no bickering
there would be no doctors, no hospitals

the object of perception appears
in a straightforward way
sounds as sounds, forms as forms

but a thought presents itself misleadingly
it is not what it stands for
in this lies its richness and its power

the thought of a person is not a person
the memory of a place, not a place
the image of rain does not make us wet
who would confuse the menu with the meal?

thought is different from a mental image
thoughts are inner words
and can express abstract things
bigger, farther, different, useless, holy

mental images are "inner pictures"
they seem close to vision
but they do not see
they imagine

to consider thoughts and mental images
as things
is a source of deep confusion

Piaget revealed this in his studies
he would ask pupils
what is heavier
the word feather *or the word* lead?
lead, *many students would answer*

or again
why is the sun called the sun?
because it is yellow
some children would answer

while early Buddhism concentrated
on perceiving the ephemeral aspect
of thoughts
the later tradition wants to understand
the very being of thoughts

to want to observe thoughts
feeds the confusion
that holds them as an objective reality
it can be a skillful way to distance oneself
from troubling ideas
but it keeps us confused about their nature

the Tibetan master Dilgo Khyentse Rinpoche taught
that in meditation on thoughts
the observer and the observed are one and the same

to be aware is not an activity of consciousness
it is its very being

watching a sunset
I can focus on the nuances
between the different shades of orange
but presence lies in being aware of seeing
not in the perception of shades of color

presence is self-consciousness
it has no object

as long as thoughts and mental images are grasped as things
they are an obstacle to presence

to recognize that we are thinking is the first step in meditation
the first return to experience
but more is required to de-thingify thought

as we have seen
thought or concept sticks to experience
if we think that our experience is good
then this goodness appears to be a quality
inherent in the experience
but it is only a judgment

similarly, when we think someone is nice
this quality seems inherent in the person

this quality of niceness appears to come toward us
as when we hear the neighbor's car engine start
we only perceive a roar
the notion of a car that starts does not reside in the noise

when I think *it's raining*
this can be true with respect to facts
but it remains an abstraction
the thought is not this specific rain with its temperature
its slant
it does not make anything wet

amazing—we believe what we think
we take our thoughts to be objective realities

why don't other people think like I do?
thoughts seem as real as stones lying by the path

to understand that what we think
is only a way of thinking
and not reality
is extremely liberating

to realize the pure subjectivity of thought
reveals its false solidity

the idea thickened, it burdens the mind which carries it:
it is a stone that can neither be lifted nor rejected
—Sartre

this is true not only of thoughts about others
but also of those about ourselves

we are not these generalizations: *I am good, I am worthless*
these are only beliefs, not realities

I am worthless: where does this thought lie?
in the head, in the heart?
inevitably we look for it
as if looking for an object
but it can't be found

by neither distancing ourselves from thought
nor losing ourselves in it
we see that it rests in consciousness
like water in water

in meditation, it is wise to maintain this awareness
not so much to convince ourselves:
it is just my mind
but to experience it clearly

emotions are linked to constraining thoughts
we can free ourselves from them
by noticing their purely subjective nature

thought is consciousness as a flame is luminosity
a thought *is* a meaning
a meaning that is aware of itself
the belief that it needs
another consciousness to clarify it
leads to a never-ending process

thus each thought reveals consciousness itself

there is no thinker behind thought
consciousness is impersonal

when we imagine people, situations
we may get irritated, we may get sad
we react as if these were real people

in a certain way
we know they are not real people
but we want to play the game

the mental image can become the place of presence
if we are free of confusion
like thought, it is not what it represents
the image of a person is not that person
it is a mental image

just as we cannot observe a thought
we cannot observe a mental image

we would have to put it at a distance
to thingify it
but consciousness cannot be put at a distance
from itself

the point is not to convince ourselves of this
but, in a certain sense, to question imagination
where is that image?
at what distance?
what are its dimensions?
life-size?
half-size?

the mental image is not seen
it is imagined
we can never discover anything new
we can think about it in a new way
we find only what we bring to it

the mental image has a meaning
it can aim at a particular person in a particular circumstance
yet it is always a generalization

is the imagined person turned to the right?
or to the left?
under which lighting?
at what time of the day?

the human ability to imagine is endless
it is very clear in the case of temporality

time is both a richness and a burden
the cement of the prison walls in which we confine ourselves

without it, there is no conditioning or progress

the image of yesterday presents itself as another time:
"the past"
yet it is only a present image
the image of the night to come
exists only in the present moment

in the same way the thoughts
before and *after*
appear not before or after
but now

the aim is not to deny time
but to free ourselves from its grip
to believe that we *have* or we *don't have* time
shows how much we have objectified it

few imaginings carry so much weight
we are stressed only by what we hold in time

strictly speaking time does not exist
yet we have to submit to it
such is our condition
we are subject to that which does not exist
but our submission exists
we are really bound by unreal chains
time which is unreal casts over all things
including ourselves a veil of unreality
—Simone Weil

the belief that we see what we in fact imagine
sustains the thingification of consciousness
and perpetuates confusion

imagination plays an important role in life, it is a resource
but here, we are interested in the being of the mental image
which is also the being of consciousness

when in meditation we catch ourselves imagining
or when images seem to appear spontaneously
they should not be treated as an obstacle
by immediately shifting the attention to the body

if the mind is sufficiently calm
it is wise to investigate the being of the mental image
and to realize that it is, in fact, that of consciousness

then, the imaginary is no longer a distraction from presence
but an aspect of presence

a Zen parable illustrates this point

one day, as he encounters a Zen master
a samurai scolds him sharply
you walk like a pig
you eat like a pig
you breathe like a pig

the Zen monk looks at him and replies peacefully
you walk like a Buddha
you eat like a Buddha
you breathe like a Buddha

unsettled, the samurai asks the monk why
he is talking to him like that

the monk explains that a Buddha sees only Buddhas
and a pig sees only pigs

a consciousness thingified by the concept *I*
sees only things
for such a consciousness,
thoughts, emotions, and mental states
can only be things

my self

I, me
these thoughts accompany most of my experiences
I am sad, I see, I walk, I think
this book is mine

the word *rose* is generic
it designates flowers of very different colors
it does not change when the flower blooms
or wilts

the words *me, I*
can be applied to many aspects of my life
that have little in common

I is the one who went to school
at the age of 5
the one who travelled at 20
and the one who is writing now

despite all the changes
physical and psychological
I has not changed

how old is *I*?
five, twenty, fifty?
I has no age, even at this moment of my life
it is only a representation

while it is useful to give a name
to this psychosomatic process
in constant transformation
to think that this *I* is an autonomous entity
completely separated from this process
is a mistake with far-reaching consequence

the word *me*, even more than the word *rose*
denotes uncountable phenomena
since it is used by each person to designate herself

me is neither short nor tall
neither intelligent nor confused
neither Western nor Eastern

what is this I who is I for me
and not-I for you?
—Aryadeva

like *here* and *there*
I is a term adrift
the same label for different phenomena

a mere convention of speech

the notion *I* weighs down all experience

it is right to say *I see*
but wrong to believe that there is an *I*
autonomous with respect to vision
vision sees, as hearing hears, as thought thinks

I is neither consciousness, nor its owner
it is a thought formed by consciousness
so that it can make a stand among things
I makes consciousness into a thing

to take this representation for consciousness itself
is the source of the deepest disarray

to relativize the notion of *I* is essential for Buddhism
its claim to resolve the problem of life and death
only makes sense
insofar as this *I*, whose disappearance I fear
is seen to be nothing substantial or independent
since it has never, really, come into being

in meditation, the aim is not to hunt the self
but to remain close to experience

when I am sad
the concept *I*
veils the experience

but if I am interested in the emotion itself
in this particular way of being for consciousness
then, in the intimacy of the experience
there is no longer a notion of self
but simply a sad consciousness

it is the same with bodily sensations
if the meditator does not cling
to an image of a particular zone of the body
or to an evaluation of the sensation
if she is not its owner
or the witness, which always implies a distancing

if she simply feels it as a way of being
the notion of self does not arise

presence is not a device of consciousness
like the *I*
it is consciousness of one's being
—*self*-consciousness—
it is necessarily impersonal

to attach the word *I* to presence
to distinguish it from other things
implies the intention to place it among things

but at the level of things there is no presence
thus presence is lost when held as I or mine

when thoughts are held as objects
they imprison us in an imaginary world
more solid than the harshest of realities

the *me*, the *I*
to which consciousness tends to reduce itself
is only the imaginary prisoner
of this imaginary world
imaginary world that is the world of generalities

as long as it takes itself to be this prisoner
consciousness will suffer profoundly
like a reader who identifies
with the tragic characters of a novel

from the three origins of the notion of *I*
confusion and pride must be eliminated
but convention must be respected

without this conventional *I*
there would be no responsibility

a play by the Greek poet Epicarmus
depicts this problem

a merchant seeks the person to whom he has lent money
to get his money back
when they meet
the person declares that
because everything constantly changes
it is no longer he who borrowed the money

surprised, the merchant thinks for a while
then smacks the debtor with a stick
the debtor, upset
asks the merchant why he is hitting him
the merchant replies that he is not responsible
because he is no longer the one who delivered the blow
and the one who received it is no longer here either

radical attempts to dispose of the self
always make a mess

exile

to mingle with the mortals, some gods of Olympus
abased themselves to take birth among humans

human beings, desiring consistency and duration
take themselves for things

to hold onto an identity
to take ourselves for a teacher, a homeless person
a waiter
is to take ourselves for an enduring thing

then we wander in endless exile
seeking ourselves among things

in this wandering, which Buddhism calls *samsara*
we have not lost our homeland
we have lost ourselves

objects are inert
they are there, but are not aware of it
while one is aware of one's being here

to make this awareness an object of observation
is to locate it at a distance

consciousness cannot be placed at a distance
from itself
anything placed anywhere
is a substitute

if consciousness is that which observes
what is observed is non-consciousness

if consciousness is what is observed
there is no other awareness to observe it

that which knows things
cannot be known as a thing
—Kant

meditation is sometimes understood as a distancing from oneself
so as to remain serene

observing different parts of the body
the abdomen, the chest
or painful sensations

means that meditation approaches bodily sensations
not as experiences
but as objects

to place oneself outside the body to observe it
is the commonest way to live in exile

as vision is consciousness of shapes and colors
bodily sensation is consciousness of warmth, heaviness
of anything tangible

to recover one's body
as a way of being
is one of the greatest contributions
of meditation

time is a construct of the mind
useful, without a doubt
it seems as stable and certain as things

a past experience
exists only as a fixed representation
it has drifted into the realm of things
it is changeless
and not self-consciousness

thus, a human in the past or the future
is nothing but a thing
it cannot perceive anything

in meditation, when we are absorbed in the past or future
we are not gone
we have drifted into the world of things

a world where there is no self-awareness
no presence

meditation then becomes an endless wandering
in search of oneself

emotions

when it cannot act on the world
consciousness transforms itself
it metamorphoses

it does not transform the situation
but its way of seeing
and lets itself be moved

this is never a fully satisfactory solution
because the emotion believes in the reality
of the appearance that it projects onto the world

thus, it is a problematic way
of facing a problematic situation

the chameleon takes on the color of its environment
but emotion changes the color of the environment
which becomes worrying, bleak, or irritating

emotions engage us with existence
it touches us through them
they are not a defect of the human condition

but they also confine us
within a biased vision of our situation
and a limited experience of ourselves

if life were as sadness sees it
how would it be possible
to not be sad?

meditation undermines the credibility of the emotion
and, finally, leads to the realization of its nature

didn't the Buddha attain enlightenment
after vanquishing the armies of Mara
after having liberated himself from the power of passions?

under the bodhi tree
he is suddenly assailed
by doubt, pride, lust
hatred, confusion

where did these armies of Mara come from
if not from his own mind?

it is necessary to recognize them
in order to vanquish them
in certain sutras the Buddha simply says
I know you, Mara

according to Buddhism
human beings are conditioned not by reality
but by their beliefs

emotion is the way these beliefs
engage human beings completely
body and mind

but these beliefs are not always conscious

I don't know why
I am constantly worried
or irritated

emotion is not a thing
it cannot be an object of observation

to dissipate all confusion about it
we must experience it intimately

it is a confusion
not of perception
but of our point of view of the world
and of ourselves

when we are depressed
we live in a lifeless world
that maintains us in depression

the anxious perceive the environment as disquieting
and lock themselves in anxiety

sadness is not what affects me
it is the way I am affected

it is not sadness
that makes me sad
but the loss of a friend

in meditation
it is important to clearly distinguish
between two faces of emotion

the emotional experience
I am worrying
and the erroneous belief that underlies it

to reveal the being of an emotion
like that of thoughts or mental states
sleepiness, kindness, or tranquility
is not simply a question of knowing
but of being

being as consciousness
as presence
not as *I*

perhaps I am initially approaching emotion
from a certain distance

this morning I am agitated
I move in all directions
by distancing myself from this agitation
I begin to acknowledge
the concern in which I find myself
I can name it

as long as an emotion remains unnamed
we cannot be present to it

once it is identified
this distance dissolves
the emotion can be intimately felt

Bion thought that the role of the mother
is to name the child's experiences
so the child can integrate them

passions touch me, they put me in touch with myself
while beliefs keep me at the level of things
of concepts like object and subject
they keep me from being present

I really feel anxious at this moment
but the belief that the world is full of danger
blurs my vision of reality
as long as the belief blurs the emotion
I cannot be fully present to it

in meditation, we can perceive
the conflation of the physical sensation
the emotion and the belief

slowly, the belief that maintains the anxiety
can be unveiled
it necessarily concerns the future
something terrible could happen anytime

but this almost unconscious vision
of an uncertain future
arises in the present, it is imaginary

when the meditator realizes this
the belief in the imminence of a catastrophe
crumbles

thus, I can feel the emotion
without reifying it
without identifying with it
like a mere aspect of awareness
finally it disappears

likewise, sadness is not what I am
it does not define me, even momentarily

it does not affect awareness
any more than a reflection affects a mirror

the solidity which the *I* would confer on emotion
dissolves

thus the emotion dissolves
into the fullness of presence
like water into water

only an impersonal presence is left

by withdrawing belief from the world
and by shifting it to consciousness
emotion loses its ground

to integrate emotion
we must shift its vision of the world
from holding it as an objective truth
to seeing it as just a belief

a boatman was helping travelers
across the upper Yellow River
when a ferry hit his boat
the boatman turned
to swear at the careless ferryman
but the ferry was empty
and his anger vanished

sadness is made up of a bodily state
of a certain vision of the world
and of the emotion
the trick is not to confuse them

a heaviness on the chest
is not sadness
the physical sensation has no meaning in itself

when each experience is felt for what it is
when contempt is seen as belief
not as truth

when sadness is experienced as consciousness
and not as a thing
the emotion is no longer burdensome
it is an expression of wholeness

during periods of intense meditations
sexual desire sometimes arises
and stubbornly persists

certain meditation manuals recommend
the use of an antidote
such as visualizing
the desired body as a bag of guts

this softens the desire
but does not reveal what it is

the practice of vipassana
tries to uncover the nature of desire

first we must identify the belief
that upholds the desire

a master of marketing
it promises more than it can give

it projects a promise of final satisfaction
onto the desired person
as if satisfaction abides there
as the nectar the bee seeks abides in the flower

when the promise of satisfaction
returns to the desiring consciousness
the meditator is no longer possessed by desire

this does not mean there is never satisfaction
but, it does not come from the object
but from the disposition of the mind
that experiences it

just as while hearing
we relinquish the notions of *I* and *car*
to be just hearing

we finally experience desire
just as a way of being

realizing that desire is consciousness
we can live it completely

we experience it as presence
and not as desire

in this completeness
nothing is missing
so what can be desired?

what is at stake in meditation
is the unveiling of the meaning of the emotion
and the discovery of its purely subjective nature

the transmutation of bondage
into freedom

oblivion

Martin Buber wonders
why at the opening of the Book of Genesis
did God ask Adam,
"where are you?"

this question concerns all of us
it challenges us
to take responsibility for our own existence

at each moment the biblical text raises the question
where are you?

endlessly preoccupied with changing the world and things
with submitting them to their own design
human beings are oblivious of themselves

they go through life
without ever raising the essential question
what is the being of the one who is constantly busy?

when meditation is considered a technique
a skill to be mastered
it simply becomes a means of projecting oneself
into the future
into the imaginary

when meditation is made to serve an ideal
the practitioner searches for himself
where he is not
in calmness and peacefulness
when experiencing fatigue, agitation, and worry

meditation becomes a place where one loses oneself

it is only possible to find oneself
within the reality of what is happening
at each moment

the spiritual path is an invitation
to reveal ourself
but it can also be a means of escape
by getting lost in an ideal of perfection
to which we aspire ever more strongly
as we try to evade ourselves

the meditator's being is at stake in meditation
if he is willing to hear the question
where are you?

to consider meditation as a technique
is another means of hiding behind an activity

Stanislavski recounts that during rehearsals
of Molière's *Tartuffe*
an actor, who had enthusiastically engaged
in the discussions about the various characters
showed great resistance to going onstage

to inhabit his character forced him to reveal himself
he preferred to hide in glib conversation

it is common to go through life
endlessly obsessing about an unfinished work

death does not attend upon our uncompleted tasks
that is what philosophy teaches us

in this endless busyness
the essential is forgotten
the very being of the one who struts and frets

meditation unveils this being
it does not require inactivity
but another way of being in action

not beyond

where is the step
just taken?

not the memory of the step
but the step itself

a step that will allow me
to take another step

an *other*
with respect to what?

a step
without past, without future
does not lead anywhere

it is not a matter of observing it
but of being the body

a body that is not without gravity

when the mind controls the body
when the mind observes it
I am fragmented

but I can be attentive
to the movement of the foot

aware of it rising
of its movement forward
aware when it touches the ground

feeling the weight of the body, slowly
shifting
resting on this foot
on this leg
on this side of the body

then, when I reach the end of the path
chosen for this walk

to feel how I am standing
how, slowly
I turn

the body can also be experienced
as a totality
as a body of presence

am I really
this body in movement?

don't I project around me
the intention of turning
that I then try to accomplish?

ceasessly hurrying to realize
the intentions that I have projected
outside of myself

where is the intention to cover
these few meters in front of me?

the intention to take a step?

the intention projected outside of ourselves
much more than ordinary thoughts
veils awareness

every one of my movements
takes place where I am

does the intention not rest within the body?

in the extending hand
in the closing of the fingers

in the turning of the body

movement requires support
that can be found only in the actual position
of the body

we can step over a line
but never over our steps

normally, you are never there, where you are
because in your mind
you are already in the place where
you are going
if for instance you change to an extremely slow rhythm
if you are really attentive
something does changes
you begin to be
where you are
—Jerzy Grotowski

during meditation in movement
it can be interesting
to explore the same gesture
repeatedly

to open and close the hand
to extend and retract the arm

repeatedly?

does the gesture leave a trace
so that it can be repeated?

when the intention and the body
are indistinguishable
the body is a body of presence

an impersonal presence

in the exploration of movement
some dancers
also discover this impersonal presence
a bare, authentic presence

which drove Deborah Hay
to renounce her role as a choreographer
and abide in an egoless state
in which the dance becomes a revelation

but meditation does not end
with this impersonal presence
as we will see

I don't sit down
to meditate
in the same way I sit down
to read a book
or drink a cup of tea

when I meditate
I don't sit down with an intention
of doing something
I don't sit to meditate
sitting is the meditation

powerless

presence over which we are powerless
wrote Maurice Blanchot
a vivid expression of what is paradoxical in meditation

deprived of all ability to do
we discover that the point of practice
is not doing but being

to place being at the heart of mediation
requires total idleness

followers of the Way, as to Buddhadharma
no effort is necessary
you have only to be ordinary, with nothing to do
—Lin-chi

activity aims at bringing into being
something that is not here

what is not here
is just a fantasy

to have a goal in meditation
even to be preoccupied with being
is to distance ourselves from being
to lose ourselves in the unreal

we cannot do anything to be present
we are always already here

we can't do anything about presence
but our capacity for absence
is unlimited

it is most amazing
that while being alive
we can choose
to be present or not to be present to our life
to take leave of life

how much ingenuity do we put into escaping
into losing ourselves in memories
in the imaginary

in anticipation of what could happen
more and more dramatic catastrophes
which never happen

a dream of a bright, endless day
which, had it been real, would be necessarily ephemeral

this is easy to recognize
but our fantasy can take the appearance of reality
touching upon an immediate,
but slightly improved experience

the same experience
a little calmer
a little clearer

not realizing that we are attached
to something imaginary
our meditation becomes lifeless

we conceive of presence
as an experience
inserted into a chain of other experiences
a tranquil, luminous experience
between the memory of the encounter I had yesterday
and my worry about tomorrow

but presence
precisely that over which we are powerless
is the relationship to the experience
regardless of whether it is tranquil or agitated

thus, we discover presence in what is here
in sleepiness, in quietness
or in agitation

we have no power over this presence
nothing has power over it
nothing can alter or improve it

there is nothing to change
nothing to transform
it is unfailingly and unvaryingly what it is
self-consciousness all the way through

we do have the power to be absent
to be present takes only a suspension
of this power

presence

the present has no history
but sometimes presence is eloquent

Stanislavski describes a meeting he had
while he was having fun with some actors
in a farm near Tula
in a village of the Russian countryside

a male figure appeared in the hallway in a peasant's coat
followed by an old man with a long beard
in a grey smock and felt boots

Stanislavski did not realize that it was Leo Tolstoy

no photograph could convey the impression he made
how can an image on paper convey the eyes that seemed to see right
through you?
they were sharp and piercing
then soft and sunny

when Tolstoy looked at anyone he became very still, quiet
he went to the heart of the man

and seemed to draw out all his inner secrets
—good and ill

if someone said something interesting
he was the first to be excited
he became youthful, expansive
and in his eyes
there was the fire of an artist of genius

presence is not an abstract thing
disconnected from the world
not an experience that requires immobility
and inner emptiness

it is rather a way of being, with nothing held back
being for oneself with the other

Yoshi Oida, the Japanese director
describes the performance of a Noh actor
in the role of an old woman grieving the death of her son

the actor expresses her sadness with so much conviction
that at the end of the play Oida cannot but seek the actor
to learn how he did do it

the actor replies that he walks slowly

this actor, certainly, lives each step he takes
not thinking of past or future
not judging the present
he simply is

the context provides sadness

responsibility

often, we are absent
outside of ourselves, almost in spite of ourselves

without effort, we remain absorbed
for long periods by a single task
yet repeated effort seems necessary
to return to ourselves

why is presence so elusive?

perhaps we only tolerate life
half-heartedly
rejecting it when it doesn't conform
to our expectations

preferring fantasy and imagination
to reality

this ability to escape into memory and imagination
is not a flaw of human beings
but an ability necessary for living

the young child needs
time to face reality
to bridge, little by little
the abyss between desire and frustration

in meditation, as in life
we still use this power of imagination
as a means of childish avoidance

ultimately, if we are not present
is it simply because we do not want to be?

the choice to be absent
is largely unconscious

when we take responsibility for this absence
we can be present

we are trying to escape
not from an external reality
but from internal conflicts

remorse returns endlessly
to the memory of a past action
that it can neither accept nor deny
it refuses to take responsibility for it

to face the event may open to the sadness
or the shame that remorse was covering
and allow for their integration

regret is not endless rumination
like remorse
but an acknowledgment and a decision
not to repeat the same kind of action
it lets us move on to something else

resentment
holds a past
that it cannot let end

this refusal keeps indefinitely in mind a memory
mistaken for the event
a memory whose imaginary nature is ignored

what would it mean to take responsibility
for an injustice suffered
other than to recognize that it has happened

when we lose ourselves in remorse
in resentment
we do not take responsibility for our past

I am not responsible for what the others have done to me
but for what I do with what the others have done to me
—Sartre

not wanting to choose, to commit
but waiting for fate to choose for me
is to refuse to engage life
to refuse to take responsibility for my future

this does not mean
that we should have control over all events
it is wise, sometimes,
to be receptive and available
with an attitude of consent, not avoidance

to accept my worry
my desire, my aversion
without denying them
without repressing them
without being defined by them
is to take responsibility for my present
is to consent to being real

conversely to play the victim
is a way of not taking life on

I could meditate
if I weren't so sleepy, so agitated
if I didn't have this need to move

as I assume my inner conditioning
as I take responsibility for it
I free myself from its constraining power

to assume means to relate it not to me
but to consciousness
to de-objectify what constrains me

responsibility subverts
avoidance and bad faith
it confirms presence

in *The Way of Man* Buber
tells a story
a disciple of the Rabbi of Lublin
once undertook a fast
from one Sabbath to the next

on Friday afternoon
he was overcome
with such a terrible thirst
that he thought he would die
he caught sight of a well
and went to drink from it

but then he realized that his inability
to hold out for just one more hour
would undo the effort of the whole past week

he turned from the well and did not drink

soon, pride stirred in him
for his ability to resist the temptation
becoming aware of the pride
he said to himself
"better I should drink
than have my heart filled with arrogance"

he returned to the well, but
as he bent down to dip his cup
he noticed that his thirst was gone

when the Sabbath began
he entered his teacher's house
crossing the threshold
he heard his teacher call out:
"Tinkering!"

Martin Buber explains
the problem of the disciple is that
he did not take responsibility for his choice
that he constantly hesitated

responsibility extricates presence
from its isolation
in passivity and disengagement
it gives presence the power to reveal itself
even in the most difficult and troubled of life's circumstances

it is revealed in all dealings with others
as it is revealed in all our dealings
with ourselves

lovingkindness

the enhancement of awareness and wisdom
sometimes seems to isolate the meditator

certain meditations cultivate an openness toward others
as well as calming the mind

numerous supports can be used to calm the mind
a colored disk, an image
breathing or a noble feeling:
lovingkindness, compassion
sympathetic joy, and equanimity

lovingkindness is the caring attention for others' happiness
compassion cares about the afflicted
sympathetic joy is the joy felt for the other's happiness
equanimity is the humility that prevents one
from presuming to govern the other's fate

meditation starts with lovingkindness
because it addresses everyone
compassion can only be concerned with those who suffer
sympathetic joy, with those who are happy

the method is simple
to feel lovingkindness emerge for one
who naturally awakens it
to absorb yourself in this feeling
and then expand it toward those to whom you are indifferent
and finally, toward those you dislike or hate

at first, we develop lovingkindness for ourselves
by wishing our own happiness
if it is too difficult
we can start with a friend

the meditator chooses a few phrases
that he incessantly repeats, mentally
trying to remain aware of the meaning
of what is being said:
may I be happy
may I be serene
may I be healthy, for example

touched by the meaning of these phrases
little by little the wish becomes sincere

lovingkindness sinks into the mind
of the meditator
then he immerses himself into the feeling
without caring about the phrases

kindness should not be forced

simply repeating the phrases
aware of their meaning
with patience, perseverance
and lightness

the feeling settles almost unnoticed
by the meditator
sometimes revealed by a particular event
instead of becoming annoyed with ourselves
we are surprised by our spontaneous tolerance
and lovingkindness

conscious that everybody
like myself
seeks well-being
that behind each decision, each action
there is a similar quest for happiness
the meditator, then, develops lovingkindness
for a friend
or someone he respects

by means of phrases like those already used
may Johana be happy
may she be serene
may she be healthy

by relating more to the meaning than the words
the wish becomes sincere

to limit the mind to phrases endlessly repeated
and then to the feeling of lovingkindness
brings calm and serenity

then, meditators direct their wishes to a person toward whom they
    are indifferent
and, finally, toward an unfriendly or a hated person
if there is such a person

if the chosen person presents too many difficulties
the meditator can go back to the previous figure
for whom it is easier to develop an authentic wish

sometimes, when the feeling of kindness
is firmly established
it is wise to let the phrases drop
with the mind solely absorbed by lovingkindness

this simultaneously engenders both a noble feeling
and a profound tranquility of mind

sometimes the mind may remain still for long periods
without a single thought
absorbed in lovingkindness
calm and serene

this does not imply an idealization
of the other
or a negation of differences
but a choice
a certain way to look at the world

the stoics did not want their happiness
to depend on what did not depend on them
circumstances, others

like that
the practice of lovingkindness should not depend
on anything outside itself
such as the goodness of others

it does not depend on the virtue of those
at whom it is directed
it is unconditional
encompassing beings both loved and hated

thus lovingkindness cannot be confused
with attachment
attachment is a conditional love
it wants to partake in the happiness of others

lovingkindness does not expect anything
it is an open attitude
it does not impose happiness on others
it simply wishes it

finally, when the practice stabilizes
the meditator sees each being
as a serene mother sees her only child
not with attachment, but with care

the spontaneity of consciousness

consciousness has no beginning
no end

a beginningless consciousness
has no before, no after
it has no duration
thus it is not situated in time
it is a pure spontaneity

a spontaneous consciousness
doesn't depend on anything
it is inapprehensible
and it is free

consciousness is not aware of itself
before or after
its present manifestation

it cannot think of
its own absence

only when we place it outside
when we thingify consciousness
can we imagine its nonbeing

then we are no longer
dealing with consciousness
but with an imaginary thing

to say consciousness is permanent
is misleading too
as it reduces it
to an abstract thing

*thus do not form any notion
about consciousness**

or about conditioned existence

*conditioned existence has no beginning
no end
it has neither before nor after*

it is absurd to force our existence
to adjust to the categories of reason
the need to be or not to be

the impossibility of grasping
our own existence
the way it flirts with nothingness
is a source of anxiety for philosophers
and the essence of freedom for meditators

---

* Nagarjuna

yet we want certainty

as we observe things
we want to observe consciousness

and thus make consciousness
like a thing

it is a persistent confusion

to reduce consciousness
to the world of things
hands it over to causality and temporality
and leaves us longing for freedom

hearing the song of a bird
seeing a cloudy sky
depends on circumstances
but not the being of consciousness

yet we constantly thingnify consciousness

to speak of observing thoughts
or emotions

to speak of seeing a mental image
when we are merely imagining

is a sign of the confusion
that takes consciousness to be a thing

I am conditioned by a past experience
because its memory
is believed to be extrinsic
to consciousness

then I am a victim
of this supposedly autonomous past
which acts like an external force

all attempts to free myself from it
are doomed to fail
if they do not de-thingify memory

sadness is a burden only when we are confused
about its nature
realizing that it is just an aspect
of consciousness
we are once again serene

sadness is itself consciousness
it does not need another consciousness
to feel it

consciousness or awareness
is not knowingness
it does not require a concept
it has no object

meditation frees us from psychological conditioning
not because it offers a space of tranquility
but because it dissipates the confusion
that takes psychological phenomena
to be things

when we realize that a memory
is a present experience
which has only the appearance of the past
we understand that it is nothing other
than consciousness itself

consciousness cannot be an obstruction to itself
as the water of a river cannot be an obstacle
to its flow
for consciousness, sadness is not
something that must be removed
like the dust that covers a mirror
it is just another thing the mirror reflects

realizing that it is only one way
for consciousness to appear
that it does not veil presence
any more than the red color of a prism
resting on a red cloth
hides the prism

only when the prism thinks it is red
when consciousness identifies with any emotion
consciousness is obscured

this simple discovery illuminates the nature
of psychological phenomena
emotions, mental states, and thoughts
and frees us from their domination

the grip of the concept must be released
a grip that solidifies sadness and worries
into things

as the cold solidifies water into ice
and makes us think
that they are different in kind

mindfulness releases the grip of the concept
allows the ice to melt into water
and emotion to be experienced
as nothing but consciousness

consciousness then regains its freedom
and spontaneity
which the emotion,
grasped confusedly
had frustrated

knowing but being

there is no reason
to be agitated without reason

the mind, left on its own
is naturally quiet

but
despite their attempts to cultivate calmness
certain meditators are endlessly overwhelmed
by thoughts or images

is more discipline what is required?

more concentration
practiced more rigorously?

certain masters insist
on the necessity to develop
concentration in the initial stage
others say it is not essential

there are two ways of calming the mind

through concentration
by firmly anchoring the mind
on a stable object

or through presence
by bringing balance to the mind itself
by not giving in to reactivity

in a monastery in the north of Thailand
I witnessed a passionate conversation
between two monks
a father and son

one advocated concentration
the other argued for mindfulness

it is a long debate
within the Buddhist tradition

some teachers think that, quite naturally
the two kinds of meditation
develop together

numerous texts describe in detail
ways to develop concentration

focusing the mind on breathing
on a feeling like compassion
on an image of the Buddha
or a sound like *buddho*

this practice is simple
some meditators
stabilize their minds easily
by an attitude that is natural for them

others need much more perseverance
they attempt to control their minds
with little success

wandering off from the object of meditation
the mind repeatedly escapes into thoughts
and imagination
that can be often futile

how to resolve this difficulty?

without knowing what triggers thinking
it is difficult to calm the mind

sometimes thoughts are simply
the effect of momentary circumstances
that generate worry or irritation

a door that we think we left open
a car not safely parked
an inappropriate remark

becoming aware of the underlying emotion
can reestablish calm

the reasons for agitation
are sometimes existential
a need to reassure ourselves, to control, to avoid

thinking so as not to feel

not moving can be distressing
for some people

thinking gives the impression
of controlling our fate

the meditator feels she must do something
she must know what is going on
she tries to hold onto any object of knowledge
unconsciously, it reassures her

she has a vague impression
that if thoughts disappear
she will find herself without markers
facing a void

in such cases
the notion of relinquishing thoughts
naturally stirs resistance

why abandon those reassuring markers?

wanting forcibly to quiet the mind
without taking into account what agitates it

can be an attempt to deny some inner reality
a reality that may be troubling

because being is ungraspable
we cling to knowledge
whose essence is to grasp

but knowing is not being

it is important not to confuse
the conceptual and the real

in his meditation manual
the master Mahasi Sayadaw takes care
to clarify this

the late tradition makes a similar distinction
not about the object, but about consciousness
differentiating being from knowing

do not place the mind inside
do not look for an object of meditation outside
let the mind rest in the meditator
consciousness itself, without doing anything
—Patrul Rinpoche

when the mind rests in itself, whatever it may be experiencing
there is no difference between
the experiencer and the experienced
between joy and consciousness of joy

between agitation and awareness of agitation

just as movement is determined
with respect to a fixed point
agitation is determined with respect to what it is not

but when there is only agitation
there is nothing with respect to which
agitation may be agitated

then there is neither calm nor agitation
simply fullness of being

when the meditator is sitting
it is not a matter of knowing that he is sitting
but simply of being

just as presence
is self-consciousness

being, is the coinciding of the meditator with herself
without the distance that knowing imposes

the meditator is simply each experience
sleepiness, calm, agitation

being as presence
not as truth

when being is left to itself
liberated from the *I*
freed from notions of truth and error
beyond being and non-being

presence, then
is without grasping, unconditioned

coincidence

meditation is the art of letting the meditator
coincide with the experience
as two circles of the same radius
coincide with each other

should we rather say *one* circle of the same radius
since there is no meditator apart from experiences

there is only experience conscious of itself

the temptation is great, then
to hold consciousness as the unique reality

certain Hindu masters affirm
that everything is nothing but being, consciousness, and bliss

a few Buddhist thinkers
go in this direction
but, generally, Buddhism does not seek
the dissolution of the subject and the object
in consciousness

it saves the meditator from both extremes
considering life as existing
and considering it as non-existing
it refrains from conceptualization

in practice
there are other means
than the unveiling of the consciousness
in each experience

Malunkyaputta, an old monk, asked the Buddha
to teach him meditation succinctly
given his old age

the Master replied that he wouldn't have other advice
for a young monk
but to leave experiences to themselves

so that
while seeing, there is only seeing
while hearing, only hearing
while tasting, only tasting
while smelling, only smelling
while experiencing bodily sensation, only sensing
while thinking, only thinking

realizing this, the Buddha continued
you will be neither here nor there
this is the end of conditioning
the end of suffering: nirvana

this way of being can be applied in all circumstances
then sleepiness is just sleepiness

agitation, agitation
worry, worry
sitting, sitting

it is not a matter of observing
not a matter of knowing
but of being

similarly, in movement
while walking, there is only walking
while stretching the arm
there is only stretching the arm

when the meditator coincides perfectly
with her experience
there is no place
there is no time
there is no language
there is only an ineffable coincidence

this coincidence manifests not only
in an empty mind
but also in the being-here
of the meditator
in her daily experiences

while drinking a cup of tea
walking peacefully on a garden path
watching the leaves turn yellow
when autumn arrives

being-here indicates the union
of the human being and the world, here

without affirming, without negating
without grasping
beyond being and non-being

then the practice is simple

fetching water and wood for the fire
cooking rice, eating a bowl of vegetables
drinking a cup of tea
and sleeping once the evening has come
as it is expressed in the Zen tradition

seeing your nature
is seeing that the willows are green
the flowers are red

nirvana is a stone

after so much wandering

perhaps we will arrive
at this sacred place in India

a place forgotten by time
and by pilgrims

a Stupa is its heart

the exuberant life of humans, of genies and plants
represented on the sandstone lintels
ends at the portico leading to the Stupa

once inside the enclosure wall
bareness and silence prevail

the Stupa is a strange monument
made of a hemispheric dome
perfectly impenetrable

to try to get closer to the center
would be vain
the impenetrable wall of the edifice
forever keeps the seeker at the periphery

symbol of nirvana
the Stupa invites the pilgrim
to enter the fullness
evoked by the dome's perfect curve
and at the same time
shows the very impossibility of this attempt

to say that God is a stone
is closer to truth
than to say that God is Goodness
as a Christian mystic once said

God could be confused with Goodness
not with a stone

should we say that nirvana is a stone
to prevent any attempt to make something of it

religious practices naturally borrow
means from the profane world
to create conditions
leading to the unconditioned

to reach the sublime state
must the meditator shed all his vices
and develop all virtues?

thus creating a conflict
between what contributes to the goal
and what opposes it

after finally reconfiguring his inner world
the meditator would reach a state
endowed with all merits
and stripped of all defects

to reach this ideal state
certain meditators
withdrawn to a solitary place
give themselves to contemplation

they gradually turn away
from everything ephemeral
secluded from the outside world
they calmly rest within themselves

they free themselves from desire, from aversion
from lethargy, from regret and doubt
by discarding the imaginary
the past and future
and by detaching themselves
from sensory experiences

taking sides neither with the pleasant
nor the unpleasant
they remain with a mind at peace

once the mind is pacified
the first ecstasies emerge
the wise disciple remains perfectly composed
without being seduced by them

having renounced everything
he will finally attain a state free from all constraints

nothing disturbs him anymore
there is nothing

is this what we call nirvana?
the unconditioned, the unborn, the deathless?

if that were the case, the unconditioned
would depend on the rejection of so many things
it would emerge only when everything has been excluded
it would not be unborn, timeless

a vision of a path
leading to the unconditioned
by a gradual removal of hindrances
is absurd

we cannot act on the unconditioned
or provoke its emergence

to do something to achieve nirvana
does not lead to liberation

to do nothing
does not lead to liberation

how to get out of this dead end?

why not start with the notion
of an uncreated nirvana

if the world is as it appears
an unconditioned freedom is impossible

if an unconditioned freedom is possible
the world isn't as it appears

any path based on causality
reifies the conditioned world
and renders the very notion of nirvana meaningless

nirvana being atemporal
meditation must be outside causality, and temporality

the practice is, therefore,
not for freedom
it is freedom itself

a freedom which, if it were the opposite
of bondage
would depend on its eradication

thus, nirvana is a cessation that ends nothing

foolish is the one
who thinks that samsara is to be eliminated
and nirvana is to be attained
—Dilgo Khyentse Rinpoche

tantric Buddhism
speaks about taking the goal as the path

Master Dogen affirms that there is no difference
between practice
and awakening

if, from the beginning there is no samsara
one will not undertake the quest for nirvana
to see one's nature
is, then, to see that the willows are green
the flowers are red
—Dogen

Lao-tzu, immobile
dries his long hair in the sun
he does not look human

Confucius gets close to him and asks
should I believe what I am seeing?
you are like a dead tree
having forgotten everything
out of this world
in absolute solitude

Lao-tzu answers
I reside at the origin of phenomena
where the mind has nothing to grasp[*]

we are no longer in the imposing presence of Tolstoy
but, perhaps, in the ungraspable presence of someone liberated

---

* Or as Longchenpa states it: "Having reached the primordial state flawless as the sky, there is no place to return to—where will I go now? Having found this point of resolution, there's nowhere to arrive. But where am I now that I am not seen by anyone?" See David Higgins, *The Philosophical Foundations of Classical Rdzogs Chen in Tibet.*

PART TWO

Reflections in Essay

thinking for oneself

A TEXT FROM THE JEWISH tradition teaches that, contrary to false prophets who use the language of another, the old, true prophets use their own language.

It is not a question of denying the past, but of taking the responsibility to keep it alive.

A commentary on Indian sutras says that tradition consists not of worshipping ashes, but of passing on the flame.

The flame of the Buddhist tradition may well be the willingness to put everything into question, even the tradition itself, something that Nagarjuna and the Sutra of Vimalakirti do so eloquently.

Thus the tradition must be seen not as a safe enclosure, but as a demand for openness and integrity.

Generally, Buddhism presents a more modern language than that of the monotheistic religions. It is founded more on reason than on beliefs.

Occasionally some Buddhist masters, in an effort to assert the universality of Buddhism, will emphasize its rationality to the point of declaring it a science. It would be wise, however, not to rush to such a conclusion.

Among the categories of Western thought and culture, Buddhism has a more natural place.

At least since the time of Socrates, there has been a current running through Western philosophy, a *philosophy of existence*, that puts the nature and meaning of human life at the heart of its questioning. Called *existentialism* in its most modern form, it includes such thinkers as Nietzsche, Kierkegaard, and Sartre.

Existentialism maintains a highly critical attitude toward science, because it approaches the question of humankind in the same way that it approaches inanimate objects, reducing everything to mathematical and geometrical abstractions.

To call Buddhism a science diminishes rather than elevates it. It diminishes man's humanity and treats him as an object, a thing.

It is worthwhile to approach Buddhism in the light of the modern world. In the past twenty-five centuries a number of discoveries have been made in the fields of psychology, epistemology, astronomy, and sociology, among others. They have changed the way we look at ourselves and the world. Would it be sensible for Buddhism to dismiss these discoveries?

In his sermons, the Buddha deeply relies on the worldview accepted in his time, as, for example in the Sivaka Sutta:

> Now when these ascetics and brahmans think that whatever a person experiences, be it pleasure, pain, or neither-pain-nor-pleasure, all that is caused by previous action, then they go beyond what they know by themselves and what is accepted as true by the world.

However, what was generally accepted during the Buddha's lifetime is not accepted in the twenty-first century. We live not in an archaic world but in a modern one—a world that has fought its way to independent thinking.

It required many brave thinkers for the Western world to extricate itself from the authority of the church. To contradict the Bible was no easy task. It took courage for scientists to unveil the discoveries that contradicted religious doctrine. Authority slowly shifted from the church to the individual. Thus was born the Enlightenment, which Kant defines:

Enlightenment is man's emergence from his self-incurred immaturity. Immaturity is the inability to use one's own understanding without the guidance of another. This immaturity is self-incurred if its cause lies not in lack of reason but in lack of resolution and courage to use it without the guidance of another.

If I have a book that thinks for me, a pastor who acts as my conscience, a physician who prescribes my diet, and so on—then I have no need to exert myself.

It is essential to think for oneself. In her book *Eichmann in Jerusalem* Hannah Arendt provocatively declares that, despite having sent millions of Jews to their deaths, Eichmann is not a monster. The SS officer is, above all, a mediocre human being with childish ambitions. What is painfully disturbing in Eichmann's case is his inability to think for himself. While monsters are rare, people unable of thinking for themselves are not. Eichmann's case shows the extreme consequences of this failure when it is co-opted by a destructive system, but it is nearly as dangerous when it is concealed behind devotion to a tradition standing for higher moral values. It is always subject to corruption.

The attitudes of certain Japanese Zen masters during the wars Japan fought in the twentieth century is a good example. These masters were considered to be awakened but they enthusiastically supported Japan's most ruthless agressions. In this case we are not dealing with naïve youths, but with monks belonging to the elite of Japanese Buddhism. Other disturbing examples can be found in the histories of Tibet, Burma, and Sri Lanka.

Isn't thinking for oneself a human being's primary responsibility? This necessity is at the very heart of the Buddhist tradition, and it represents one of the most salient traits of its modernity.

To think for oneself is important, but is it enough? Arendt's view of the Eichmann case is compelling but raises new questions. Certainly

Heidegger must have known how to think for himself, yet he supported the Nazis during the war. Isn't the ability to empathize necessary even for philosophers?

Vimalakirti's teaching declares that wisdom without compassion is bondage.

Doesn't empathy, at least to a certain extent, defend independent thinking against arrogance and moral error?

Independent thinking can also be blind, when it seeks to ignore its own shadow areas.

When we rush to call Buddhism a science or a philosophy rather than a religion, we neglect important aspects of the tradition and it becomes difficult to properly evaluate rituals and meditative experiences.

Science, focusing on the naïve beliefs of religion, reduces it to a kind of proto-science and ignores its higher aspect: the inconceivable. It is easy to understand why, since science has no access to this inconceivable.

When Buddhism enters into dialogue with neuroscience and philosophy, it confines itself to the level of thought, the second source of knowledge. When Buddhism chooses art as its interlocutor, as in dance, poetry, or the art of Zen gardening, it privileges inner experience—life, not ideas.

During the Buddha's lifetime, a people called the Kalamas lived in a small town situated on an important trade route. Numerous masters and preachers of all kinds stopped in the town, praising their own doctrines and condemning others. Each one was convinced he possessed the truth. As a result, the townspeople did not know whom to trust. When the Buddha visited, they sought his help. His answer was clear:

> It is normal, Kalamas, that you should have doubts and be perplexed, because doubt was born within you for a reason.
>
> Kalamas, do not let yourselves be guided by sayings or by traditions. Do not let yourselves be guided by the authority of

the religious texts, simple logic, or allegations, appearances, or the thought "This religious person is our spiritual teacher."

When you know of yourselves that certain things are wrong, blameworthy, condemned by the wise, and that when you put them into practice they lead to wrong-doing and misfortune, abandon them.

We can assume that when the Buddha questions the authority of religious texts he has the Vedas in mind. But now that his own words are regarded as religious texts, shouldn't they be questioned as well?

Buddhist Sutras are not revelations transmitted by a prophet who received the words of God—they are more or less faithful transcriptions of the Master's words.

It would be strange if the Buddhist philologists were to take each word of the sutra as truth, while contemporary Jewish and Christian commentators endeavor with great honesty and courage to question the authenticity of every section of their holy scriptures.

Although the Sutras are an extremely rich source, we must not over-estimate their importance. I remember asking a Burmese master what he thought of a certain well-known but problematic Sutra. Without a moment's hesitation he replied that this text was not authentic, thus resolving the problem perhaps a bit too easily.

The Pali Sutras certainly represent one of the best sources of knowledge of the Buddha's teachings, but they cannot be taken literally; they do not excuse the followers from thinking for themselves.

In the Sutras, the Buddha often replies to various questioners and his answers are given according to the context, the questioner's tradition, and the time the Master has at his disposal.

Sometimes the context forces the Buddha to answer in a nutshell. For example, when he is about to leave for the neighboring village to collect alms, an ascetic suddenly appears and presses him to answer. The Master tries to postpone the exchange, but unsuccessfully. At last he is forced to respond succinctly yet without loosing his clarity.

The Sutra may describe the context, but the circumstances of its compilation are also significant. In which community did they appear and which doctrinal opponent is the aim of the Buddha's teaching? Numerous Sutras appeared after his death. Certainly these texts do not present the Master's own words. They nonetheless significantly enrich the Buddhist tradition despite advancing sometimes contradictory points of view.

It is said that Irenaeus, the Bishop of Lyon, aware of the contradictions appearing in the four gospels, asserted that they would give worshippers food for thought.

The Buddha's first biographies are rather late, and seem to be motivated by hagiographic concerns rather than historical ones. Indeed, we know very little about the Master's actual life.

It is striking that, at the beginning of Buddhist art, the Buddha was represented by an absence: an empty throne, a footprint, a stupa, a wheel, or a tree. This absence of the Master seems to suit his doctrine well. It is centered not on his person, but on an inner experience to which each follower is directed, an unconditioned experience.

When the Buddha's faithful attendant Ananda hears the news of the death of his guide Shariputra, he despairs. To answer his anguish, the Buddha doesn't offer his help, but in the Cunda Sutta he urges Ananda:

> Shariputra has not taken anything you would miss. Be a refuge, an island for yourself. Take the Dharma as a refuge, take the Dharma as an island. Do not seek other refuge.

In other words, he sends Ananda back to his own authority. To be one's own refuge means to be fully present in each moment without grasping to anything.

But to continue the spiritual quest beyond mere calmness demands a strong determination for freedom.

It is difficult for a tradition to reconcile the necessity to preserve and to perpetuate the teachings of its founders with the breath of rebellion and freedom that initiated it. It is a challenge to prevent the letter from killing the spirit.

Didn't Nietzsche, the proclaimer of God's death, claim that had he been born in the time of Jesus he could have been one of his disciples because in them lived a spirit of revolt and contestation?

The great Sufi Hallaj said: "I am the real." When asked "What is the real?," should one of his disciples answer "Hallaj," he would provide the perfect example of treason against the spirit.

A Japanese master, more concerned by the spirit than the form, affirmed: "I am not looking for the masters of the past, I am looking for what they were looking for."

morality and suffering

THE MEANING OF SUFFERING is one of the most troubling questions.

The Buddhist tradition approaches it in two different ways: initially through the law of karma, and then through the notion of a chain of conditions. Over time, the second way gained more and more importance in the Buddhist doctrine. By including the intention of the agent in its conception of karma, from the beginning Buddhism integrated a psychological consideration into the search for the cause of suffering. This notion was mostly absent from the Jain and Brahmanist ideas on the subject. But, with the chain of conditioning, Buddhism offers a much more developed psychological description, which gives a clear understanding of suffering and highlights individual responsibility. The theory of karma does this only indirectly and less coherently. It is surprising that these two visions have continued to coexist and that the notion of karma has been preserved in spite of its dubious aspects. Is this because the theory of karma is more likely to motivate the practice of generosity and lovingkindness, for example, than is the chain of interdependence?

Two sutras illustrate those different points of view. One describes the succession of lives under the influence of karma; the other, the chain of conditioning.

When the Bodhisattva had attained concentration of mind, from which all bonds had been abandoned and exhausted, a mind which had become perfectly pure, taintless, supple and easy to direct, which remained firmly in place, he knew his previous existences, one birth, two births . . . thousands of births . . . all the while thinking: "I, in times past, was born in such a place, was given such a name, belonged to such a clan, ate such foods, led such a life and span of life. I felt such pleasures and pains. Having died, I was reborn in another place. Dying again, I was reborn in yet another place." He knew the facts of innumerable previous existences lived in these differing ways. When, during the first watch of the night, the Bodhisattva achieved this initial understanding, ignorance ceased and knowledge appeared with the clear vision of previous existences.

Thanks to his perfectly pure divine eye, he saw the births and deaths of beings. Examining them, he knew that beings whose actions of body, speech, and mind were bad, whose opinions were false, who criticized and denigrated the saints, these beings, when their bodies were destroyed at the end of their lives, fell into hell or were reborn among the animals and hungry ghosts.[*]

On the other hand, the sutra specifies that beings whose behavior was exemplary were reborn in heaven or among humans.

Another sutra, describing the chain of conditioning, affirms:

When a disciple of the Buddha has seen correctly the chain of conditioning as it really is, it is not possible for him to turn back to the past thinking: "Was I or wasn't I in the past? What

---

[*] Quoted in André Barreau, *En suivant le Bouddha.*

was I in the past? What was I like in the past?" Or, that this
disciple turning toward the future asks himself: "Will I or
won't I be in the future? What will I be in the future?" In the
present moment, he cannot ask: "Do I or don't I exist? What
am I, where do I come from, and where am I going? "Why
can't he think this? Because this disciple has seen the chain
of conditioning correctly.

—Paccaya Sutta

This chain of conditioning, or chain of dependent origination, is
particular to Buddhism, while the law of karma, slightly revised, is bor-
rowed from Brahmanism or more probabily from the Jaïn and presents
numerous difficulties.

Buddhism divides phenomena into obvious phenomena, perceptible
through the senses; hidden phenomena, accessible through reason and
meditation; and extremely hidden phenomena, knowable only through
faith in the words of the Buddha. Karma belongs to this third order; to
adhere to it depends more on faith and obedience than on intelligence.
The chain of interdependence, however, can be known directly.

For orthodox Buddhists to challenge the law of karma is taboo. It
takes considerable daring to conform to the doctrine only selectively.
It is different in the Hindu tradition, at least from the point of view of
the great thinker Shankara, who, true to his philosophy of nonduality,
does not hesitate to question the law of karma. Would Buddhism lose
its depth without this notion? This is doubtful.

Thus Buddhism teaches two skillful ways of seeing the world. One
view, the notion of karma, is mundane, tainted, because it rests on the
notion of a self. At best, it can lead to a fortunate rebirth, but not to
freedom from samsara.

The other, unbiased view does not rest on the notion of a self. On
the contrary, it reveals the unreality of the self. It depends mainly on
a clear vision of the chain of conditioning, which enables one to reach
enlightenment.

In one sutra, the wandering ascetic Sivaka questions the Buddha on a theory defended by some ascetics, according to which all sensations felt by an individual, whether pleasant or unpleasant, depend on his past actions. The Buddha asserts that there are other causes of suffering as well. Besides karma, there are bodily organic disorders due to the winds, bile, and phlegm, and there are external circumstances such as bad weather, seasonal changes, and accidents. Thus the notion of karma plays an important part in Buddhism, but one has to be careful not to overestimate its magnitude.

The term *karma* stems from the Sanskrit root *kri,* which means "to do, to act."

This notion first appears in the Vedic tradition, where rituals hold a major position. Rituals aim at inducing the gods to act for the good of the performer or of the person for whom the ritual is being performed. The Vedic gods intervene in human destiny. It is important to perform the ritual in the appropriate manner, not committing the slightest mistake in its celebration, lest the gods turn against the performer. In this context, "bad" karma is merely a ritualistic error; it has no moral implication.

When Buddhism inherits the notion of karma, it cannot assign it the same meaning.

For Buddhism, the Vedic gods are insignificant, no longer endowed with power over human life.

The notion of karma, for Buddhism, concerns the moral value of actions done intentionally. Good karma is action undertaken to benefit oneself and others. Bad karma is action undertaken with the intention of harming oneself or others. Happiness and joy are the fruits of good action, while suffering and difficulties are the consequences of bad action. In this notorious breach with the ancient Vedic tradition, humans have freed themselves from their dependence on the gods: they have become responsible for their own destiny.

Thus one view of karma leads to greater responsibility and freedom, while another, rigid view leads to fatalism and the absence of liberty.

In the Tibetan language as well as in Sanskrit, the terms used to designate karma and causality are different. To question or to negate the law of karma doesn't imply the negation of causality, as some authors seem to fear. In Tibetan, for example, *las*, the equivalent of the Sanskrit *karma*, means activity, action, and work. The term *karma* means action, specifically a willing, conscious action.

What, then, is karma? According to the master Vasubandhu: "It is the willing and what is produced by this willing."

Thus the law of karma is not merely a principle of causality. It is a particular type of causality—a moral causality. To reduce karma to psychological conditioning makes it more understandable but overshadows its problematic aspect. An apple falling from a tree or a heavy storm doesn't respond to the law of karma, as it is not led by an intention.

If this way of considering karma appears to be richer than its Vedic sense, it is not without its own difficulties. Without of the power of the Vedic gods, where is the force to steer destiny? What hand will direct the arrow?

To ascribe karma wholly to the workings of natural law is also problemaric. Just as a wheat seed does not give birth to a rice shoot, a bad action does not produce a happy fruit. But a natural law suffers no exceptions. It leaves no room for choice, and thus no room for morality.

One can imagine social, psychological, or legal causality, but moral causality isn't plausible.

The law of karma is based on presumptions that must be questioned: What need does it respond to? Justice demands a culprit to be punished, but what do ethics demand? Traditionally karma is presented as a law, not imagined by the Buddha but observed by him.

Since Kant's Copernican revolution in philosophy, we no longer believe that laws are part of nature, but that they are the projections of the scientific mind and its need for landmarks. It truer still in morality, where we can never observe any incontestable fact.

According to Buddhism, only the superior knowledge of the Buddha can perceive the law of karma. It wouldn't be a problem if this law didn't present so many inconsistencies. For example, the law of karma implies that the fruit of generosity is abundance. But between the generous act and its abundant result it is hard to see a link other than the magical. There are traditional texts that attempt to quantify the link with rates of return.

In the Abidharma Kosha, Vasubandhu specifies:

> If one person gives to an animal, the donor will receive a fruit a hundred times superior to the gift; if he gives to a human being he will receive a fruit a thousand times superior to the gift. Even though they are not nobles, the fruit of the offerings made to one's father, to one's mother, to a sick person, or to a teacher, is immeasurable.

Plato was satisfied with a mere tenfold return on his moral investment.

For an experience of suffering to expiate an act of wrongdoing, there must be equivalence between the two, equivalence that seems impossible to demonstrate. What do they have in common? What suffering expiates what wrongdoing? When the parents of a murder victim demand the perpetrator's head, we can sympathize with their desire for vengeance but we cannot say that their attitude is moral. Yet it is what the law of karma requires. The law of karma is based more on the impulse for revenge than on observation of facts. It promises a violent death as a consequence of murder. It can serve to protect society, but does it hold up morally?

The story of Angulimala shows the ambivalence of Buddhism with regard to the law of karma:

An assassin lived at the time of the Buddha. He emptied the cities and the countryside of their inhabitants. One day, the Buddha was returning from his alms round and turned onto the path leading to where Angulimala, the murderer, was spreading terror. The local shepherds vainly attempted to dissuade him from continuing on his way. When the bandit saw the Buddha, he decided at once to kill him. Armed with his sword and his shield he started chasing after him. But the Master used his magic so that Angulimala, who was running with all his strength, could not catch up with him, as he walked calmly. The frustrated Angulimala ordered the Buddha to stop. "I stopped long ago, Angulimala, it is you who must stop," said the Master. Impressed, the murderer stopped in his tracks, threw away his sword and shield, and became a monk. Thanks to his practice of meditation, he attained nirvana.

It is hard to imagine a more burdensome past, but it didn't prevent Angulimala from attaining liberation.

If the birth of a deformed child is an injustice, who is guilty? In such a case, the notion of karma appears to provide the semblance of an answer. But in reality, the notion that the deformity is a consequence of past actions creates more problems than it solves. To say that the child or his parents are responsible for this disability is not only arbitrary but also cruel.

What, then, motivates adherence to the doctrine of karma? Morality would seem to favor magnanimity over the need to see the culprit suffer. A god may forgive, but not karma.

In the Buddhist tradition, one can analyze profound questions such as selflessness or emptiness. But to question the law of karma is much more difficult as it does not depend on reason.

In the Kalama Sutta, the Buddha boldly considers the possibility that actions bear no moral consequence.

> Now Kalamas, the noble disciple, whose thought is unspoiled and pure, free from hatred and malevolence, finds the four certitudes, here and now:
>
> "Let us suppose that there is a world after death, that there are fruits for actions good and bad. If that is the case, then it is possible for me to be born after the dissolution of the body, after death, in one of the heavens where the celestial happiness is." This is the first certainty.

"Let us suppose that there is no world after death, that there are no consequences for actions good and bad. Still, here and now, in this lifetime, I remain safe with a happy thought, freed from hatred and malevolence." This is the second certainty.

"Let us suppose that bad results fall upon the individual who committed bad actions. As far as I am concerned, I don't wish any harm to anybody. How could it be then that a bad fruit falls upon me, as I am not doing anything harmful?" This is the third certainty.

"Let us suppose that bad consequences don't befall the doer of bad actions. As a consequence, in both cases, I find that I am pure." This is the fourth certainty.

Thus, a virtuous action maintains its value whether or not there is karmic consequence.

The Sivaka Sutta formulates in an interesting way the origin of the mundane view. Noting that not all feelings depend on karma, the Buddha said:

You may know through your own experience that there are sensations caused by bile, as well. The existence of sensations originating from bile is generally recognized as true. In such a case, O Sivaka, religious people and Brahmans who say "All sensations, agreeable, disagreeable, or neutral, experienced by such or such an individual, depend on his past actions" go too far from the fact that we can know through personal experience and from facts generally recognized by the world . . .

Concerning karma, the Sutta goes on:

You may know through your experience that there are sensations produced by the ripening of actions. The fact of the existence of sensations that originate from the maturation of actions is generally recognized by the world as true.

We have to take the popular belief into account. The law of karma, in one way or another, was held to be true at the time of the Buddha. This mundane notion is then regarded as right view. At this point, the reasoning becomes circular: the Buddha adopts the law of karma because it is accepted by the world, and centuries later his followers adopt the law of karma because it is taught by the Buddha.

But the Master does not restrict himself to perpetuating what the world regards as true. At the heart of his teaching is the absence of self, and this teaching is far from being regarded by the world as true.

It is easy to understand the practical importance of a law of ethical causality to help a community of people to live together, whether this community be lay or monastic.

But does it make sense?

Plato uses skillful means to show the relationship between wrongdoing and suffering, benevolence and happiness. He uses myths to motivate people to virtue.

In *Between Past and Future,* Hannah Arendt remarks that we may not know if Socrates believed that ignorance causes evil and that virtue may be taught, but we know very well that Plato thought it wiser to rely on threats.

At end of the *Republic* Plato tells the story of Er, a warrior who died on the battlefield. For ten days he was believed to be dead, but then he came back to life to tell what he saw.

Er was slain in battle, and ten days afterwards, when the bodies of the dead were taken up already in a state of corruption, his body was found unaffected by decay. On the twelfth day, as he was lying on the funeral pile, he returned to life and revealed what he had seen in the other world.

He said that when his soul left the body he went on a journey with a great company. They came to a mysterious place where there were two openings—in the earth and in the heaven above. In the intermediate space there were judges seated, who commanded the just to ascend by the heavenly way on the right hand; and in like manner the unjust were bidden by them to descend by the lower way on the left hand. As he drew near, they told him that he was to be the messenger who would carry the report of the other world to men, and they bade him hear and see all that was to be heard and seen in that place.

He noticed that some souls coming up from the underworld were covered with filth and others coming down from heaven were pure. All these souls were headed for the plain to establish camp. And they told one another of what had happened by the way, those from below weeping and sorrowing at the remembrance of the things which they had endured and seen in their journey beneath the earth, while those from above were describing heavenly delights and visions of inconceivable beauty. He said that for every wrong which they had done to anyone they suffered tenfold and the rewards of beneficence and justice and holiness were in the same proportion.

Almost all religions have such stories. In Christianity the most famous is perhaps the story of Teresa of Avila. For three days she was considered dead. Her eyes had already been covered with wax, her absence of breath checked with the help of a mirror. But her father, who loved his daughter deeply, could not bring himself to authorize her burial. Suddenly, on the third day, she opened her eyes.

Such stories are known in Tibetan Buddhism as well. Chadgud Tulku, a contemporary master, describes in detail his mother's narrative after she came back from her journey in the netherworld. These stories are consistent in asserting some form of judgment that the dead face in the hereafter.

This transactional attitude is far from a spiritual path.

Nietzsche declared: "I would be wary of a person who would need a reason to act virtuously."

Parents who abuse their child have often been themselves victims of abusive parents. Some combat veterans use violence to manage their anxiety. They are violent as a consequence of the violence to which they have been subjected.

The law of karma has to be grasped with the prudence necessary to grasp a snake. Otherwise, instead of leading to responsibility, it will lead to fatalism and to loss of freedom.

Perfectly aware of this danger, the Buddha in the Tittha Sutta describes three types of belief that lead to the abandonment of all responsibility: the belief in a God who determines human destiny; the belief in absence of any causality, where everything that happens is the product of chance; and the belief in a distorted notion of karma, which holds that all present actions are determined by past actions, so that murder, theft, and betrayal can all be chalked up to past karma.

Sartre, using a modern language, says something quite similar:

> If we define man's situation as one of free choice, in which he has no recourse to excuses or outside aid, then any man who takes refuge behind his passions, any man who fabricates some deterministic theory, is operating in bad faith.

As an alternative to these three flawed notions, Buddhism proposes reflection on what conditions an experience to be felt as painful. The "Sutra of the Two Arrows" describes the part played, not by karmic conditioning, but by the attitude toward the present experience.

This sermon teaches that in one sense there is no difference between an ordinary man and a skilled disciple: both encounter painful situations. Yet they have opposite reactions. When an ordinary man feels pain, he laments, he complains. He looks for escape in sensuous pleasures. It is as if the ordinary man, after being hit by a first arrow, were sticking a second arrow into himself.

On the other hand, the skilled disciple doesn't complain, doesn't lament when she experiences suffering. She doesn't look to sensory pleasures for escape; she knows of other ways, and so she doesn't stick another arrow into herself.

By dodging suffering, the ordinary man misses the opportunity to know the nature of the experience, whereas the skilled disciple, who does not resist the experience, knows its nature and knows the conditions that allow it to arise and to disappear. Ignorance and wisdom are what set these two apart, and what differentiates samsara from nirvana, conditioning from liberty.

It is said that Rabia, the great mystic of Islam, used to walk around Baghdad carrying a torch and a bucket of water. She wanted to burn paradise and drown hell, so that the faithful would not pray out of hope for paradise and fear of hell.

Marguerite Porette, the great Christian mystic, said one should pray without a why.

What would the practice of virtue lose if it did not bear fruits? A virtuous action undertaken without concern for future gain or spiritual advancement but simply for its own sake. This virtuous action would receive its value not from expected consequences but from the liberty it expresses. Virtue would gain in depth and freedom.

This view is, of course, not foreign to Buddhist tradition. It has a number of formulations. Two types of generosity and morality are described in the great treatise of wisdom attributed to Nagarjuna. One is pure and the other is impure. Generosity and morality are impure when they are motivated by the hope of gain; they are pure when they are not motivated by the hope of gain.

It is not certain, then, that the notion of karma is useful. We cannot say that people behave nobly in countries where the law of karma is taught, and ignobly where it is not. The importance of the action is ascribed to its supposed future fruit rather than to its present actually.

Moreover, it is not certain that the practice of virtue for its own sake is less engaging, as the theory of karma is never totally convincing.

A lover of liberty will be careful to avoid passions because they contain their own negative retribution. The absence of desire, hatred, and confusion is already freedom. No additional benefit is needed.

To think that without the belief in karma humans would have no motivation to restrain their passions is both naïve and cynical.

There is no point evoking here an ultimate attitude based on emptiness; rather we are concerned with a very simple level of reflection concerning daily activities. The motivation is neither happiness nor progress, but freedom, which cannot be served by passions.

The solution to the problem of suffering is to be found in suffering itself.

According to the "Sutra of the Two Arrows," the attitude toward the present experience is determinant.

If the causes of my present suffering were situated in the past, they would remain inaccessible. I could do nothing about it. I would remain forever the victim of my past. Whoever or whatever holds the key to my suffering, to my conditioning, holds the key to my freedom as well. Freedom can be only in the present or it will remain forever a dream. The challenge lies within my relation to the present experience. It doesn't mean that the past has no impact; it has an impact not as past but as a present memory.

According to Anna Freud, it takes a double shock to cause a trauma: a real shock and an imaginary one. The real shock is past; it no longer exists, whereas the imaginary shock abides in consciousness, acting up.

Psychoanalysis and psychology have made remarkable progress in unveiling the source of "ill being" in many persons and in showing the means to free oneself from it. The traces of forgotten life events, often from early childhood—unexpressed emotions (desire, hatred) or traumatic ordeals (separation, deprivation, violence)—are at the root of many difficulties. By deciphering these traces, some people can free themselves from that which prevents them from fully being.

Here is an example given by the child-psychoanalyst D.W. Winnicott, in *The Sense of Guilt*: A five-year-old girl reacted to the death of her father, which happened in extraordinary circumstances, by falling into a deep depression. The father had bought a car when the little girl was going through a phase where she both loved and hated him.

When he proposed to take the family for a drive, she begged him not to go. He ignored her pleas, got into an accident, and flipped the car. The little girl was the only one who walked away unscathed. She went to her father, who was lying on the road, and kicked him to wake him up. But he was dead.

Winnicott notes:

> I was able to watch this child through her serious depressive illness in which she had almost total apathy. For hours she stood in my room and nothing happened. One day she kicked the wall very gently with the same foot that she had used to kick her dead father to wake him up. I was able to put into words her wish to wake her father whom she loved . . . from that moment she gradually came back to life, and after a year or so was able to return to school . . .

In a meditative process, it is not unusual that the image of some painful events, long forgotten, come up to consciousness. This is an important phase in the spiritual path of some people. They will need to use all their meditative sensitivity and equanimity to live the emotions linked to those memories, but without being overwhelmed, without letting themselves be reduced to those emotions, and without identifying with them.

If we believe that the past determines the present, personal effort becomes pointless. Responsible behavior gives way to fatalism. Rather than succumbing to karmic determinism, Buddhism rigorously analyses psychological causality. It certainly presents the first development of an elaborate psychology. But it is not an "ego-psychology"; quite the contrary. The psychological analysis of conditioning aims precisely at showing that the chain of conditioning is not governed by a self, that it is an impersonal process. This naturally leads to the deepest level of right view, the ultimate level. The outcome of this vision is the eradication of a belief in an independent and real self.

In the present moment, says the Paccaya Sutta, the wise disciple cannot ask: "Do I or don't I exist? What am I, where do I come from, and where am I going?" Why can't he think this? Because this disciple has seen the chain of conditioning correctly.

When difficulties or hindrances appear, when the meditator is, for example, paralyzed by worry or overwhelmed by sorrow, to invoke the notion of karma to justify this condition would prove not only useless, but harmful. One has to be aware of the complexity of the present experience, to be aware how the belief, the physical sensations, and the emotion condition each other. The Kalaha Vivada Sutta describes this chain:

> Where do controversies and quarrels, suffering, distress, arrogance come from?
> Tell me!
> Quarrels and arrogance happen because the human being is subjugated by objects and people.
> Where does this subjugation come from?
> Desire, anger, ingratitude, and doubt are the source of this fascination.
> Where do they come from?
> From the notion, "It is pleasant, it is unpleasant."
> How do those notions "It is pleasant, it is unpleasant " come about?
> They come from experiences (contact). Without experiences, they would not exist.
> Where do experiences come from?
> They come from the body-mind!

We might say, they come from being-in-the world.

This chain of conditioning is binding when it happens without the subject's knowing it, but when there is awareness, at that moment, another choice—freedom—becomes possible. It then becomes possible not to react compulsively when there is an agreeable or a disagreeable sensation, but remain in equanimity. Without identifying with the attachment or the aversion that might appear, the meditator liberates herself from their binding power. The chain of conditioning is thus broken.

This chain can be broken only in the present. For Saint Augustine the freedom of human beings is precisely this capacity to break away from the chain, a capacity to start anew, a capacity that is the essential characteristic of human nature, which animals do not have. This freedom allows human beings to change the course of events, to step out of the chain of determinism.

This wisdom, this awareness, leads not merely to virtue but to freedom.

It is necessary to differentiate consciousness from knowledge, as we will see. We should not simply recognize or name, but experience.

In the Satipatthana Sutta, which most extensively describes the practice of meditation, the Buddha calls simply for awareness. When a meditator is troubled by desire, he is conscious that his mind is troubled by desire. In other words, we have to bring to our consciousness what is agitating us without our knowing it.

Samsara and nirvana aren't places like hell and paradise, but two different attitudes toward life. One is confused and servile; the other is awakened and free.

In the later form of Buddhism known as Mahayana or the Great Vehicle, a more mature attitude arose, shifting from an ethic of retribution to an ethic of responsibility and, finally to an ethic with no object. This it does by means of the deepening of the notions of love, compassion, and emptiness.

Shantideva, the master of the development of altruism, gives many judicious and rather convincing arguments to motivate the practice of compassion.

I am responsible for the happiness and protection of others because they are not different from me.

In contemporary thinking as well, such as from Sartre, we find reflections shedding light on the relation to others:

> Thus, the first effect of existentialism is to make every man conscious of what he is, and to make him solely responsible for his own existence. And when we say that man is responsible for himself, we do not mean that he is responsible only for his own individuality, but that he is responsible for all men.

Later, Sartre says: "Our responsibility is much greater than we may have supposed, because it concerns all humankind."

Those words may be inspiring, but they don't compel responsibility. There are no criteria, as strange as it may appear, to support the justification of morality. If altruism were justified by a benefit I could expect, it would be egocentrism. If it were the compliance with a duty, it would be mere obedience.

In the street, when I meet a beggar asking me for help, what can justify my response?

What right do I have to say no?

What would convince me to give something?

It is useless to look for a reason for my choice. There is none.

I am solely responsible for the sense I give to my freedom. Yet my responsibility is at stake, as my choice determines the world in which I live: a world in which a beggar is taken care of, or a world in which people in need are completely ignored.

consciousness

BUDDHIST TRADITIONS address the question of consciousness in a number of ways. The Burmese are particularly interested by its ephemeral aspect; the Tibetans engage in minute analysis of its various aspects and also meditate on its deeper nature. In this chapter we will follow mainly the Tibetan tradition.

The Chinese take a more global approach. In order to talk about consciousness, they use parables and metaphors such as the story of the meeting between Huike and Bodhidharma.

> Huike said to Bodhidharma: "My mind is restless. Pacify it."
>
> Bodhidharma replied: "Bring me your mind and I will appease it."
>
> Huike: "Although I looked for it exhaustively, I could not find it."
>
> "Here you go," said Bodhidharma, "I've pacified your mind."

Is consciousness unknowable?

This seems to be the point of view shared by Kant, who states that: *what knows the object, cannot be known as an object.*

If something escapes knowledge, what kind of existence can it have for us?

Terms such as *consciousness, awareness, soul, mind,* and *presence* will be used here with a similar meaning according to the context or the source.

But the terms *consciousness* and *knowledge* should not be taken as synonyms.

In the West, the term *consciousness* originally had only a moral meaning, until Locke related it to *self-consciousness.*

In Tibet, lamas debated the definition of consciousness for centuries. The main point of disagreement was whether consciousness could know itself directly, without the mediation of a concept.

As it will be described below, the use of concepts is precisely how to distinguish knowledge from consciousness or awareness.

Therefore, the question really centers on determining whether consciousness is accessible through knowledge or must be approached some other way and what that way would be.

This is important not only for the meditation on consciousness but for any kind of meditation. Is the meditative mind (awareness) bound to knowledge and thus to the limits of rationality where being and non-being are mutually exclusive, or is it beyond such limits, where affirmation and negation have no meaning?

INVESTIGATION OF CONSCIOUSNESS

For the great Indian Buddhist thinker Dharmakirti:

> Objects are apprehended by means of an imprint that they leave on the consciousness by means of sensory organs. Therefore, when the consciousness perceives external objects, in reality, it gets to know itself.[*]

The purported external world is known because consciousness is

---

[*] Georges Dreyfus, *Recognizing Reality.*

conscious of itself and interprets its own transformations as signs from the external world.

In ordinary experience, knowledge gives meaning to the impact that affects consciousness: it sets an outside world facing the subject—"I." Knowledge is interpretation.

A consciousness that is reduced through knowledge to a thing set in front of a thing, is stuck in a world of things; is a soulless consciousness.

Knowledge is a particular mode of relating to the world. It transposes all experience, all perception into data that can be preserved in memory, classified, and transmitted. The concept is the means of interpreting experience.

Each experience, each impact is singular, incomparable, whereas a concept is a generalization.

The term *rose* can be applied to a multitude of different flowers. Even if we were to be more precise and say *a red rose*, or a *rosebud*, these would still be generalizations. This is precisely the nature of concepts. It must generalize to communicate and to evoke numerous analogous experiences for people using the same language.

The concept endures; the experience, however, does not.

Knowledge that I am sitting stays, but the awareness of being seated fades as soon as my attention is directed to something else, such as a sound.

Nothing could be compared to the sunset that I see now. No other sunset will have such clouds, such silhouettes of trees in the foreground, such nuances of red and orange.

I cannot compare two perceptions because they can never manifest at the same time. Only similar things are comparable, like a memory to another memory. When I compare the present perception to an earlier one, which is no longer present, I transform the present experience into a concept.

Knowledge is generalization, clustering. It puts a veil over experience. Knowledge sets the object as being separate from it, precisely as *ob-ject* (thrown in front). If the object is indeed what sits in front, it must face something. In this face-to-face both protagonists must belong to the same domain, unlike a crow and an owl which can never meet either by night or by day, to take a classical example from the Tibetan tradition. Only a phenomenon that shares characteristics with the object can hold this position, characteristics such as to be discernable and localizable.

Could consciousness take this place?

Some Buddhist masters have defined consciousness as "that which knows an object." In other words, there is always an object, and thus consciousness and knowledge are identical.

But this definition does not include a consciousness of consciousness. For the proponents of this definition, consciousness cannot know itself directly, like a knife that cannot cut itself.

However, to describe a consciousness that can know an object without being aware of knowing the object seems incomprehensible. Sartre came to the same conclusion:

> . . . for if my consciousness were not conscious of being consciousness of the table, it would then be consciousness of that table without being so. In other words, it would be a consciousness ignorant of itself, an unconscious—which is absurd.

For those Tibetan thinkers who do not distinguish between consciousness and knowledge, between awareness and knowingness, consciousness can only be "known" through the mediation of a concept.

This implies knowledge of an anterior moment of consciousness. In line with this vision, certain manuals of meditation suggest either to focus on the memory of a moment preceding the present moment, or to use one part of consciousness to focus on another part of consciousness. But past moments exist only as concepts for the present mind.

Thus this type of meditation leads not to a direct experience of consciousness, but only to the grasping of a substitute.

But the substitute cannot be conscious of anything; it is not consciousness but a substitute. It does not have the lucidity of consciousness but rather the opacity of objects.

Because the definition of consciousness as "that which knows the object" does not include self-consciousness, it has been rejected by many Tibetan thinkers.

The traditions of Theravada Buddhism also differ in this respect. Generally, the Burmese think that consciousness cannot know itself directly, as a finger cannot touch itself.

In Thailand, the forest tradition has yet another point of view on the subject. From Ajaan Maha Boowa:

> In the normal waking consciousness of the meditator at this level of practice, the knowing presence is fully aware of itself, aware that the mind and the knowing are one and the same timeless essence.

What is clear and knowing is a less restricting definition of consciousness and more widely accepted by Tibetan masters. They have, however, enlarged the meaning given to knowledge so as to include a consciousness that is a nonconceptual self-consciousness.

In each experience, in each perception, consciousness knows something, and, at the same time, it is conscious of being conscious of something. But consciousness is not posited as a specific object, as is required for knowledge. In *Being and Nothingness*, Sartre calls this a "non-positional consciousness of itself":

> Every conscious existence exists as consciousness of existing. We understand now why the first consciousness of consciousness is not positional; it is because it is one with the consciousness of which it is conscious.

This idea is not new. As Saint Augustine said: "The mind does not know itself as in a mirror."

One encyclopedic dictionary of philosophy (*The Dictionary of Untranslatables*) states:

> Many medieval philosophers conclude from this theorem that, despite the claims of Aristotle and the Peripatetics, the soul cannot know itself in the same way that it can know other things, namely through representation or abstraction, and that it does not know itself either as another thing or as another soul. It knows itself as self-presence, and in, through, and as that self-presence.

This means that, for consciousness, to be is to be conscious of itself.

MEDITATIVE APPROACH

In the Buddhist tradition, two types of meditations are practiced. The first approach—*samatha* (tranquility)—aims at calming the mind through the development of concentration and it uses knowledge—that is concepts or mental images.

The second type of meditation—*vipassana* (insight)—is based mainly on the meditative presence called *sati* so as to unveil the being of consciousness and of phenomena.

The practice of vipassana, like that of mahamudra of the Tibetan tradition and Zen, aims at freeing consciousness from grasping and thus allow this unveiling.

The practice of concentration does not pose problems of understanding, since this aptitude is amply developed in everyday life. Indeed, some stability of mind is more or less a necessity in the accomplishment of daily activities.

To improve concentration, a simple technique can be used: the meditator chooses a particular object and keeps it in mind.

The meditator can focus on breathing, or on a positive emotion like compassion. She can also recite a mantra or fix her attention on a colored disk or the flame of a candle.

Concentration does not rely on the perception of an object which is in a constant flux, but on the mental image it leaves on the mind.

Without respite, each time the mind loses itself the meditator comes back to the chosen object. With time and after much practice, the meditator can stay concentrated on the object for hours, without any fluctuation.

Concentration has a goal: it requires effort. It presupposes the orientation of attention toward a specific object. The object of concentration, which is conceptual, casts a shadow over presence.

Imagine a tennis player. He is perfectly conscious of the grip on his racket, of the position of his opponent, of the exchange, of the movement of the ball, fully conscious of everything that happens during the game, but he may completely forget himself. This is an example of concentration, of attention, but without presence.

At a certain level of concentration the concept of I disappears, but not the object of concentration.

For example, a meditator practices concentration for several weeks. He fixes his mind from sixteen to eighteen hours every day on a yellow disc, avoiding all fluctuations of the mind, all deviation toward other objects such as sounds, ideas, or bodily sensations. His mind being solely concentrated on yellow, he reports that one day at breakfast as he saw the yellow yolk of an egg, he felt like he was being swallowed by it— he was about to disappear. At this stage, there is no longer any presence.

We can notice this in daily life. When we are completely absorbed by reading, by doing our taxes, or in the contemplation of a landscape, consciousness becomes completely absorbed by its object. At this moment self-consciousness, even of the I (its substitute), fades. There is no longer a manifest I. Only the landscape persists.

This fusion with environment is probably the initial state of consciousness, the state of the infant. Then the child develops his capacity for knowledge. He learns to name, to differentiate, to grasp. Thus, when he wants to apprehend himself, he naturally follows the mode of grasping the objects. His surroundings also teach him to differentiate himself from objects by objectifying himself. His mother cannot perceive the consciousness of her child—she perceives only the outward manifestations of his emotions and his moods. Thus, she will also objectify him through the notions such as *you* or *I*. He apprehends his own presence by means of a substitute—the concept *I*. But the *I* is placed at the level of things. It does not have the transparent clarity of self-consciousness, but rather the opacity of an object, precisely because it is not self-conscious.

Self-consciousness represents an extreme state of maturity for a human being, a state that can only be acquired slowly and never definitively. The construction of the self that is involved in this process will be discussed in the following chapter.

Sometimes in meditation the concentration naturally disengages from this confusion and moves toward the abandonment of the object. This can be the case when the conceptual object of concentration is linked to perception, as in breathing. Indeed, to be attuned to this process it is necessary to feel the bodily sensations. As the consciousness becomes uninterested with its object, the concept is naturally abandoned. Only perception lingers and then only consciousness. Again returning to Maha Boowa:

> At the same time, the breath— which is coarse when you first begin focusing on it—gradually becomes more and more refined. It may even reach the stage where it completely disappears from your conscious awareness. It becomes so subtle and refined that it fades and disappears. There is no breath at that time—only the mind's essential knowing nature remains.

In the meditation which leads to insight, we need to break away from the need to interpret and remain at the level of self-consciousness. This is a subtle meaning of the practice of sati, of presence or mindfulness.

The eighth-century Indian sage Shantarakshita wrote:

> A mind that is by nature one and without parts cannot possess
> a threefold character; self-awareness thus does not entail an
> object and an agent as real entities.

The meditator, by resting at the level of being and not of knowing, is fully in each experience which, without being circumscribed by the notion of *I*, is wholeness. As it is said in the Sutra: while seeing, just seeing, while hearing, just hearing.

The meditator will need to transcend this wholeness, not to fall into negation, into the void, but to free herself from the notions of being and non-being.

Then the practice becomes truly vipassana—insight, clear seeing. It does not pertain to knowledge, which necessarily relies on concepts, but to awareness.

In meditation this fundamental aspect of self-consciousness can appear to be so pervasive, that some Buddhist thinkers question the reality of the external world. Only consciousness is real for them.

Understanding, however, that this view brings more problems than solutions, most Buddhist philosophers reject this point of view.

We are so used to grasping an object through some characteristics that we want to do the same with consciousness. But any characteristic is a meaning given by consciousness.

The definition of consciousness cannot reveal it. Attachment to any concepts, even the one that defines it, still veils it.

The more I cling to the interpretation that I make of an experience—the table as an object of my perception—the less consciousness is going to be unveiled.

Consciousness does not distinguish itself from an object by objective aspects—it does not possess any. If it had its own characteristics, it could not take the appearance of knowable things. It would be locked in its own way of appearing. Consciousness cannot get out of itself: when it imagines a thing outside of itself, the image is nothing but an appearance of the mind. There is nothing else to compare it to. It has no position, and, therefore, there is nothing in front of it.

Knowingness, on the other hand, does position something in front of it, and, therefore, it must position itself. It can inhabit a position in front of an object only by endowing itself with characteristics that are relevant to objects. This thingification of consciousness takes place in knowledge, by means of the concept I.

This *I* is essentially the representative of the consciousness at the level of things. Sartre offers a clear description of the process:

> Everything happens, therefore, as if consciousness consti-
> tuted the ego as a false representation of itself, as if conscious-
> ness hypnotized itself before this ego which it has constituted,
> absorbing itself in the ego as if to make the ego its guardian
> and its law.

Perhaps it would be wiser to say that knowledge constitutes a false representation of consciousness because it depends on representations to grasp at anything.

The I is the host of consciousness—it is not the owner.

Thus we have an opposition of two concepts: subject and object. The duality can never be a duality of consciousness/object, but must be a duality of two phenomena of the same order: two things circumscribed by knowledge.

To say that the object is facing consciousness is absurd because consciousness has no position.

To consider a *knowing* of consciousness, Indian Buddhist philosophers define two types of knowledge that do not necessitate conceptual mediation.

On the one hand, there is a consciousness that is conscious of itself and that is not dual. On the other hand, there is a mode of *knowing* that depends on the practice of meditation, called yogic perception. It is a consciousness freed from knowledge rather than a type of specific knowing.

Thus, for this system, consciousness is *knowable* not through knowledge, but through self-consciousness.

This kind of nonconceptual knowledge is what we call vipassana. According to Mahasi Sayadaw's *Manual of Insight*:

> In order to develop true insight knowledge, starting with knowledge that discerns body and mind, one should observe ultimate mental and physical phenomena and not conceptual objects.

In Theravada Buddhism, the practice of meditative presence is called *sati*; somewhat similar practices, such as mahamudra or Dzogchen in the Tibetan tradition, or zazen in Zen, allow the unveiling of consciousness to itself.

Sati, literally "to remember," is understood in different ways. It can mean to remember the consequence of positive or negative action, or the object of concentration, or, in the context of insight, it means the presence of consciousness to itself.

Here we will consider the second meaning in our approach to meditation.

The choice of the term *to remember* to express this self-consciousness or presence is not surprising. To remember something, one has to have been present when something earlier happened. If, for example, I am given a list of groceries to buy, my presence at that moment will allow me to remember the things I need to purchase. If I was distracted at that moment, I would not remember anything. Sati is that which allows us to remember.

Saint Augustine wonders wether memory is also of things that are present.

But someone will say, that is not memory by which the mind, which is ever present to itself, is affirmed to remember itself; for memory is of things past, not of things present . . .

And therefore as it is called memory in things past which makes it possible to recall and remember them, so in a thing present, as the mind is to itself, that is not unreasonably to be called memory, which makes the mind at hand to itself, so that it can be understood by its own thought, and then both be joined together by love itself.

The difference between concentration and insight (vipassana) is fundamental. Through concentration, the mind focuses on an object—it is preoccupied with content, it stays fixed on something that it knows. Concentration requires grasping, and this can only be done by means of concepts. In Sanskrit and in Tibetan, the term to "grasp" is part of the term that expresses concentration (Skt.: *ekagrata*; Tib: *ting nge 'dzin*). In vipassana, and especially in the kind that leads to realization of the nature of consciousness, the mind rests in itself. The difference between concentration and meditative presence is not a question of the difference of objects, where we would change one object for another.

In meditative presence, in the sense that it is meant here, there are no specific objects. Rather, there is a different attitude.

Ultimately, we must let go of knowledge for consciousness to unveil itself in any experience, be it either perception, emotion, or thought.

Because consciousness is not an object, its exploration calls for an unusual approach. There is a recurrent tendency to fix it among the objects of knowledge. But here it is not a question of knowing, but of being. Sartre writes:

In no case could my consciousness be a thing because its way of being in itself is precisely a being for itself. To exist is for it to have consciousness of its own existence.

As Shantarakshita, the eighth-century Indian master, puts it: "Consciousness, contrary to things, is immaterial and conscious of itself."

An objective is that which we are endeavoring to attain; it is not present and is, therefore, imaginary. Consciousness cannot be the object of a quest. What the quest would aim at would be a non-present consciousness, or a nonconsciousness. Hence all desire, all hope to discover what consciousness is, would be a vain illusion.

To unveil the being of consciousness, one needs to be without intention, to stop wanting what is absent or wanting the disappearance of what is present. Meditation must be free of all objectives, simply to be with the present experience. Residing beyond intentionality, meditation leaves science and psychology for the mystical or, simply, for an inner experience.

A science devoid of intention is meaningless. Neuroscience never captures consciousness. It only detects its physical traces; this is obvious to most researchers. Scientists will always remain like a hunter that sees only the traces of the animals he tracks. The study of these traces can certainly be useful, as witness the progress that it has led to in the treatment of Parkinson's disease by the use of electrical stimulation in the brain.

But the emphasis on cerebral imagery in the investigation of consciousness is surprising and reductionist. Why ask the brain what consciousness is but not ask consciousness itself?

Wanting to situate consciousness in the brain at all costs is a bias that must be brought to light.

An image can illustrate this impossibility of ascribing a location to consciousness. Imagine a screen on which a film is being projected. The film shows a winding mountain road and, on the right, a lake. Where is the screen situated within this landscape? In front of the mountain, behind it, next to the lake? This question is obviously absurd as the screen cannot be situated anywhere within the image it shows. But don't certain scientists look at the landscape to find consciousness? Aren't they looking for consciousness among its creations?

To enter into the non-language of consciousness, one must be daring. One must be willing to let go of the desire to know. It is in the unknowable that consciousness reveals itself.

"Leave behind the thought and the thinker, let the mind be carefree like a small child," taught the Indian master Saraha.

How does consciousness reveal itself in vipassana meditation?

WHILE PERCEIVING

There is no satisfying theory of perception. All of them present certain difficulties.

Buddhist tradition affirms that the initial stage of perception is not conceptual; it poses no object. This self-consciousness, which perception is essentially, is simply conscious of the impact of the external world upon it. Then, almost immediately, a concept is linked to it. The concept represents the phenomenon in an approximate way, lending a general sense of its characteristics, but does not convey its singularity. Holding to the concept gives the illusion of duration; its very imprecision allows a sense that it does not change from moment to moment. But the concept, unlike the mind that holds it, is powerless. The word *dog* does not bark.

The difference between perception and conceptualization can easily be understood with the following example. When I enter into a coffee shop, I think I am seeing the coffee shop totally and not only a part of it. I can make a 45-degree turn, then a 180-degree, and I will still have the impression of seeing the same coffee shop. But what I actually see is totally different.

In imagination and in perception (at the second instant, when there is interpretation) the concept is the same, but the motivation cause is different. Perception is determined by external phenomena, by the sense organs, and by intention. Imagination is governed by purely subjective factors. At the first moment of perception, consciousness is nondual, impersonal, and atemporal. It is unable to retain anything.

If it were possible to make perception itself recur, then the past could become present.

From Sartre's *The Imaginary:*

> Alain, among many other philosophers, has shown well that judgment rectifies, organizes, and stabilizes perception. The passage from "something" to "this object" has often been described in novels, especially when they are written in the first person. "I heard" says Conrad, for example "muffled and irregular noises, crackings, cracklings: it was the rain."

According to Dharmakirti, the great psychologist and logician of Indian Buddhism, due to the speed of the mental process, the untrained person usually cannot differentiate conceptual from nonconceptual cognition. Only on special occasions, such as some form of meditation, can a clear differentiation be made.

One can then make a clear differentiation between concepts and the bare, unelaborated impressions conveyed by the senses.

For Mahasi Sayadaw the function of eye-consciousness is only to see visible forms, not to ascertain physical gestures or movements. However, succeeding mental processes follow so quickly that ordinary people think that they see, as if with their real eyes, the movement known by the succeeding mental process of investigation.

Meditation makes it possible to experience the first instant of perception before the emergence of the concept and the separation between the subject and the object. This means that consciousness is not yet circumscribed by the notion I, the substitute that represents it. It is thus revealed to itself in an obvious and nondual way.

Through practice it is possible for an experienced meditator not to fall into the conceptual world, either by remaining in the attitude of the first instant, or, when a concept emerges, by not referring to it, to remain free from it. This requires the suspension of all intention. These practices are described as much in early Buddhism, as in its later developments.

At Kalaka's park, the Buddha tells the monks that he knows everything there is to know in the universe. Everything that can be known by various beings, gods, demigods, priests, and ordinary people, he knows. The Buddha wants to make it clear that he does not suffer any deficiency.

He continues by affirming that, while seeing, he does not construct an object seen, an object to be seen, or a seeing subject. While hearing, he does not construct an object heard, an object to be heard, or a hearing subject. Similarly for the sense of touch. He does not construct an object touched (the body, for example), an object to be touched, or a touching subject. And so on with the other sensory realms. Finally, when the Buddha thinks, he does not create an idea to be thought, or a thinker.

The experience coincides with itself: while seeing, there is only seeing, while hearing only hearing, etc.

This sermon describes precisely the meditative attitude. It evokes, much more clearly than the Satipatthana Sutra, the way to transcend knowledge that relies on the subject/object duality.

It is not about knowing, but about being.

In *Flight of the Garuda*, a Tibetan text of the nineteenth century, Lama Shabkar guides a meditator to realize the way distance is created, separating the subject from the object:

> Try to determine where the mind goes when it moves.
>   Through which sensorial door does it leave the body?
>   When it reaches the environment in a blink of an eye,
>   Does the body move too?
>   Or is it only the mind?
>   Study this precisely.

In a sermon, Meister Eckhart teaches the following:

> When that which the five senses have dispersed returns to
> the soul, then she has a power in which it all becomes one.

This is where the purity of the soul lies, in which she is purified from a life which is divided and enters a life which is unified.

This is not another orientation of the mind inward, but rather a suspension of intentionality: an abandonment of the primacy of knowledge in favor of awareness.

In his sermon on poverty, Meister Eckhart teaches that true poverty is not having anything, not wanting anything, not knowing anything.

WHILE THINKING AND IMAGINING

How does consciousness reveal itself while thinking and imagining?

We conceive of the world of thought in the same way as we construct that of object, in the opposition of a subject to an object. In the field of perception, this opposition seems obvious—there is a world there, in front of the observer. It is surprising to find the same kind of vision concerning thought: a thought situated in front of a thinker. This means that we give thought concrete existence. All attachment to a point of view, an opinion, an idea, presupposes, in one way or another, a naïve belief in a certain reality of thought, that thought exists, in the way a tree or a rock exists.

Jean Piaget asked children whether a word had any power. "Yes, it does," a child answered. So he asked him to give an example. "The wind," the child answered. But why does the word "wind" have strength? Because it travels fast, the child answered. For children, words and thoughts both exist on the level of things.

Generally, the naïve attitude sees in thoughts independent phenomena, the meaning of which must be uncovered. I follow my thoughts like the sentences in a book. They precede the consciousness that I have of them. But a thought is consciousness, awareness of a concept, not the concept itself. It is akin to hearing, not to a sound.

A book conveys concepts, not thoughts.

Freud is also was aware of this confusion about the nature of thoughts:

> It may sometimes happen that a hyper-cathexis of the process of thinking takes place, in which case thoughts are perceived in the literal sense of the word—as if they came from without—and are consequently held to be true.

One of the essential characteristics of thought is that it can pass itself off as what it is not. Thought does not take itself as its own object. It intentionally aims at something else. If I am thinking about a person, I target that person and not the thought of that person. Perhaps I remember that I should transmit information to this person. But I have nothing to say to the thought of this person.

I can imagine my house in the countryside and all the work it needs. I am not aiming at a thought, but at an object. But what I take to be a concrete object does not possess the transparent nature of consciousness.

In all knowledge, consciousness takes on the opaque appearance of an object, whether it is real, like a mountain, or imaginary, like the next appointment. This is not a flaw, but rather the very process that allows us to set forth a world and to communicate with one another.

For consciousness to be aware of itself, it must suspend interest in the object: not to push the object away, but to stop making it the center of interest. Through this shift, the mental image or the thought is no longer held as a thing, but experienced as self-consciousness, as presence. Now consciousness no longer has a thought, it is the thought. It *is* the thought as self-presence. When there is no more goal, no more intentionality, the subjective pole, the thingification of the mind through the concept I, disappears. If the appearance of the object is still present in the mind, it no longer appears as a separated object; it is appearance as self-consciousness. Then if this appearance disappears, only self-consciousness remains.

Whether there is appearance or not, it has no impact on self-consciousness.

Thoughts have no color or shape, but this is also true for sounds, tastes, smells, and tactile sensations. A thought is empty of shape, but not of meaning.

The meaning of a thought does not require another moment of consciousness to be understood: it is the aspect under which self-consciousness manifests itself at that particular moment. Consciousness itself is that very meaning. Similarly, the mental image means something; it is the aspect through which self-consciousness manifests.

The mental image of my friend does not show *him*; it means him. It does not have the possibility of a variety of perspectives that seeing offers, but it has the certainty that it does not mean anybody else.

To demonstrate this principle definitely, certain Tibetan texts proceed with an exhaustive analysis of the mind, leaving out no possibilities.

First we must realize the intangible nature of thoughts and mental images, not to take them for things. If they existed concretely, it would be possible to locate them, to determine their origin, their trajectory, their location. But when we search for thought in this way, we do not find anything. The mental image of a mountain does not come from a mountain. A mental image of a person does not come from the person; in fact, we can still imagine a person who is no longer alive. When I think of a friend, the image of this friend is neither here nor there; it does not have dimension; it cannot be localized. An image of somebody who is in front of me is situated nowhere—it is not in my head or in my heart. It has no counterpart, no *other* with respect to which it could be positioned.

The mental image is essential to intention. An ancient Tibetan meditation manual describes the way to guide a disciple to become conscious of the nature of the image at play in intentionality. The teacher tells his student to walk toward a rock situated at some distance. Before the student reaches it, the teacher stops him and tells him to come back. Then he asks the student where the unaccomplished part of the walk is.

For the Theravada, it is not so much a question of recognizing the nature of the intention but of becoming conscious of the way it conditions action without necessitating the intervention of an independent agent, an I.

I cannot discover anything new in the mental image. There is only that which I imagine.

The French philosopher Alain notices that it is impossible to count the pillars of the Pantheon from the image of it retained by memory.

In this way, the meditator frees herself from the naïve belief in the objective reality of the mental image.

Consciousness cannot be divided; it has no temporality or spatiality. For consciousness there is no before or after or now. Nothing is outside of the mind because it has no inside or outside—it is a totality.

This is what is revealed by the Tibetan meditation.

A meditator should search for thought just as he would search for an object. Does it emerge from the mind, does it remain within the mind, does it dissolve into the mind? To inquire into the origin of thought is to place it outside. It is already treating thoughts like things. The analysis concludes that if thoughts arose from the mind, we would have two sorts of consciousness: that which emerges and that from which it emerges, that which remains and the place where it remains, and so on. Does thought emerge from the previous consciousness or the present one? If it is from the previous one, there would be no contact between the two instances of consciousness; past and present do not coexist. If the thought emerged from the present consciousness, then we would have two kinds of consciousness.

This inquiry leads the meditator to drop this type of investigation.

Thought is not spatially situated. There is nowhere to direct one's mind. As Patrul Rinpoche says:

Do not place your mind inwardly. Do not search for an object to meditate upon outwardly. Rest in the meditator, mind itself, without fabricating anything.

When the intentionality of consciousness is suspended, the mind is conscious of itself in each experience, in each perception, in each emotion, in each thought and imagination. It is no longer distracted by its own creativity. The relaxed mind rests within itself.

There is no effort to direct consciousness toward something concrete. There is just letting consciousness rest and be aware of the present mind, fresh and detached.

EMOTIONS AS AWARENESS

It is difficult to define the emotional aspect of consciousness. Not so long ago, William James, reversing the conventional order, claimed that we are frightened because we run, or that we are sad because we cry.

Despite his many astounding discoveries, Freud sheds very little light on emotion. In fact, instead of "emotion," he prefers using a term which is translated into English by "drive," which evokes a force, an energy. When he speaks of desire, he is preoccupied with its fate, but not with what it actually is. Then, he mainly sees gratification, repression, and sublimation as possible resolutions of desire. Freud knows what desire does or what we do with it, but not what it actually *is*. Treating drives like objects, like forces, he cannot understand their integration into consciousness because it is precisely the objectification of a drive that prevents its integration. Only things of similar nature can be integrated.

Thus, when mystics or yogis talk about detachment and oneness, Freud conceives this only as repression and regression, not integration.

Bodily sensations, difficulties in breathing, heaviness on the chest, or a stomach ache exemplify ways that emotion engages the whole of the person. But since it has no meaning in itself, the bodily sensation is not the emotion.

A skillful means to deal with the sensations, such as tension, knots, and so on, is to disconnect them from the associated emotion. Thus, the bodily sensations are integrated in the body. This is a way to break the loop which holds sensations, beliefs and emotions together.

Emotion pertains to the sphere of consciousness; therefore it is conscious of itself. It is unnecessary to become conscious of sadness or worry. A sadness that would not be conscious of being sad would make no sense at all. It could not be felt. There is no difference between joy and consciousness of joy.

This does not mean that it is recognized, that it is named. It is consciousness, but not yet an object for knowledge.

Something disturbs me and I don't feel very well. Then, suddenly, I can put a name on the feeling: it's sadness. I feel it before I can name it.

Emotion is essentially a way that consciousness has of dealing with a situation in the absence of a concrete solution. The mind tends to alter its vision of the world and its affective state when it can no longer act upon the world.

For sadness, the world is bleak; for worry, it is menacing; and for desire, it is full of promises.

In the words of Boileau, "Each passion speaks a different language."

Emotion is not that which touches us, but the manner in which we are touched.

Sadness is not that which affects me, but the way that I am affected by, say, the loss of a loved one. Sadness cannot be integrated if it is not seen through the belief that structures it.

Therefore, introspection is sometimes necessary in order to recognize that we are in the grip of an emotion. Taking some distance from what is felt can be wise. When an emotion such as sadness persists, that's easy. But sometimes an emotion can be more diffused and harder to name.

A teacher described how his meditative practice was laborious for a long time because he did not fully apprehend the troubles that had befallen him. He was taking his feeling for irritation, when, in fact, it was worry. When he finally managed to identify it, he no longer had any problems to be present to it—the emotion had become perfectly integrated into his meditation.

There are two steps to dealing with emotions. First we need to realize that the way we look at the world is not objective, to recognize that it is a creation of our mind. But to merely think it is not enough; we need to see it. Then the emotion can be integrated into the consciousness, experienced as self-presence, as awareness.

When we are angry, we try to reason with ourselves and thus change our point of view. Then the consciousness presents itself differently— as more calm, more peaceful. Anger has disappeared. This is the most common way of dealing with emotions. We have transformed the way we look at the world but have not realized that this way was imaginary.

Sometimes, however, the emotion is no longer connected to the memory of the event that provoked it, and so it is more difficult to discern the belief that arose from that event.

The second step aims at de-objectification of the emotion, so that it can be experienced as a way of being, as a presence and not as a foreign body. This is the process of integration.

To be present to an emotion without objectifying suspends momentarily its coercive power, but it does not touch on its meaning. It is also important to understand the belief that structures it.

Let's suppose that a person is worried. Something troubles him, but he does not know what. Little by little, through the images that appear spontaneously during his meditation, he discovers that this worry is due to a memory of an event that happened in childhood. For two hours, he was lost in a forest. To this day he holds the belief that he needs to be found, but without knowing it clearly. The event is outdated. The best way to render noncredible the old belief that he must be found is to confront it with present reality.

Anger is a means to avoid feeling helpless. It conceals our distress like the ink that a squid uses to conceal its flight. It appears clearly in the scream of a child that tries to avoid the feeling of helplessness when he is confronted with the lost of his all-powerful feeling. Anger always appears after the event, when there is nothing else to be done, never before. Perhaps it also carries sadness as a component, even though it may pass unnoticed. To open oneself up to the feeling of helplessness that underlies anger is a wise way of giving life to a process which, until now, was frozen, and may finally lead to an integration of anger.

In an odd way, a story found in the suttas illustrates how not to objectify something that is purely subjective: While the Buddha was begging for food, he knocked on the door of a house. A Brahman opened the door. As soon as he saw the Master, he insulted him. After some time, the Buddha interrupted him and asked him what happens when a person refuses a gift he is offered. Whom does the present belong to? The Brahman answered that the gift belongs to the giver. So it is, the Buddha continued, with the insults that you are offering me. I don't want them. Keep them. They are yours.

Here the Master gives two lessons: one on forbearance and one on the process of projection.

Why bring an end to the desire by satisfying it, if the desire itself is pleasant? What is desired is the satisfaction that is projected onto a particular object. Its nature is imaginary. In meditation we withdraw into the mind what was believed to belong to the objective world.

I remember the way my teacher, Geshe Rabten, described desire. He insisted that the satisfaction we see in an object is a projection, a creation of the desire itself. He gave examples of two people receiving an old Citroën car as a present. One person was satisfied, while the other, hoping for a bigger car, was disappointed. He concluded that if satisfaction were found within the object, the satisfaction that the two people experienced should have been identical.

To realize that desire falsely locates satisfaction where there can be none, that satisfaction is to be found in the mind only, greatly weakens the grip of desire. By changing the way we look at things we affect the emotion.

Then that emotion is experienced as self-consciousness, as presence.

This implies a letting go of the need to grasp that generates the subject/object dichotomy, and thus the emotion is experienced within the intimacy of a nondual consciousness.

The objective pole is the dull aspect that sadness projects onto the world, or the dangerous aspect that anxiety projects onto the world. As long as we believe in the reality of the vision affected by emotion, we are trapped in confusion.

The subjective pole is the reification of self-consciousness through the concept I or me. I am so angry. This point will be developed in the following chapter.

When there is no more identification, the emotion is naturally experienced as self-consciousness. There is only this emotional consciousness left, in its totality. For example, desire is then experienced as pure presence, as wholeness. Desire loses its impulsive drive, which was a condensation due to the objectification of desire. Without having been satisfied, suppressed, or sublimated, it resorbs naturally into consciousness.

In *Flight of the Garuda*, Lama Shabkar describes precisely the analysis of emotions in order to eliminate the belief in their objective reality.

He recommends that the meditator think of people who have hurt him in the past. He suggests that we clearly remember this, to allow anger to surface and to observe it. Where does this anger come from, where is it at this moment, and ultimately, where does it go? Then check whether this anger has a color or a shape. When observed in such a manner, it is seen to be empty. There is nothing to grasp and, without rejecting the anger, we free ourselves from its grip.

Lama Shabkar then advises us to clearly imagine a seductive person, succulent food, beautiful clothes that make desire emerge. Then, observe this desire: where does it come from, where is it situated at this moment, and, finally, where does it go? It is important to determine whether this desire has a color or a shape. When the meditator investigates thus, she discovers that there is nothing to grasp. Without rejecting desire, she de-objectifies it and frees herself from its grip.

THE BODY AS PRESENCE, AS AWARENESS

In a sermon the Buddha refused to answer the question of whether the body and the mind are distinct or identical.

It is not so much the philosophical, but the practical aspect of this question that is of interest to us here. In meditation, Buddhism places great emphasis on the body, not only to show its ephemeral or impure nature, but also as the privileged locus of presence, a presence in the unity of body and mind.

The Satipatthana Sutra invites the meditator to be aware of each position, of each movement of the body.

When a meditator is standing, she is aware that she is standing; when she walks, when she stretches or folds her arm, she is aware; when she eats or drinks, she is aware. The Sutra enumerates all kinds of movements and activities.

Munindra, a twentieth-century Indian teacher from Bengal, taught that if a meditator is sitting and he knows that he is sitting, then he is meditating.

But the term *knowing* is problematic. It is difficult to imagine that a person can sit without knowing it. It may be better to say that a person is aware of sitting, aware of stretching an arm, of turning the head, and so on, or that a person is present in the movement. When a person knows that she is sitting, even if other experiences emerge, she does not lose this knowledge. But when a meditator is aware of sitting, if thoughts do emerge, at this very moment, the awareness of sitting disappears.

Knowledge is as lifeless as things of the past—awareness, or presence, is life in its totality.

But what does it mean to be present in a movement? It is not that we should observe the movement or the sensations; this would lead to knowing. Here we need to be, not to do, to be this presence in movement.

Being this movement of the arm, but being as a totality, gets the person in the game. It is being standing, not holding oneself up.

Some dancers speak of "a body of presence" in order to avoid this body/mind dualism.

Even though it is impersonal, this body of presence is individual. The notion of I would bring the bodily presence back to the opacity and limitation of a concept.

Position and movement are ways of being, if they are not subjected to a goal, or recorded by the mind. This does not stop them from being useful, but it takes away the predominance of utilitarianism.

The Bhagavad Gita expresses it this way:

> He who sees the inaction that is in action, and the action that
> is in inaction, is wise indeed. Even when he is engaged in
> action he remains poised in the tranquility of the absolute.

During walking meditation, one walks forth and back without going anywhere.

By taking away all goals, all usefulness, the discovery of being in every movement is enhanced. But this can also be experienced in a useful activity if the agent does not lose himself in the goal.

As dance or theatre become disengaged from the critical gaze of the audience, their art comes very close to certain aspects of meditation. They can shed light on essential aspects of meditation in movement through the originality of their research and language.

Eliade affirmed that the sacred is the place of the densest presence. Therefore, the quest of a dancer or an actor partakes of the spiritual.

Jerzy Grotowski tells his actors:

> When I say that the action must engage the whole personality
> of the actor if his reaction is not to be lifeless, I am not talking
> of something "external" such as exaggerated gestures or tricks.
>
> This act of the total unveiling of one's being becomes a gift
> of the self which borders on the transgression of barriers and
> love. I call this a total act.

Grotowski sheds light on the notions of vulnerability and sincerity that are rarely evoked in texts on meditation.

He would challenge his actors about what they wanted from their lives—whether they wanted to hide or to reveal themselves. For him, if a person learns how to do something, she does not reveal herself, she reveals only her skill.

Jerzy Grotoski:

> We arm ourselves in order to conceal ourselves; sincerity begins where we are defenseless.
> Not to hide simply means to be whole.

The status of the body is ambiguous. Unlike the eye, which does not see itself, and the ear which does not hear itself, the body perceives itself. It is simultaneously the organ of perception and its main perceived object. It is at the same time the subject for me and also an object for me and others. The gaze that I can cast on my body, this way of making it an object, distances myself from it. With respect to my body I adopt a point of view of others, the same values criteria where appearance prevails over being.

A Buddhist text says that when he experiences a bodily sensation, the Buddha does not create an object to be felt, or a subject that feels: while perceiving, there is only perceiving.

From the Kalaka Sutta:

> Thus, monks, the Tathagata, when seeing what is to be seen, doesn't construe an [object as] seen. He doesn't construe an unseen. He doesn't construe an [object] to-be-seen. He doesn't construe a seer.
> When feeling the body, he doesn't construe a body sensed, a body to be sensed, he doesn't construe an experiencer.
> When cognizing what is to be cognized, he doesn't construe an [object as] cognized. He doesn't construe an uncognized.

He doesn't construe an [object] to-be-cognized. He doesn't construe a cognizer.

The sensation is not what is to be experienced, but the experience itself.

It is surprising that there is so much disagreement on the subject of consciousness, because its unveiling is the human experience that presents the highest degree of evidence. This evidence comes from the fact that it does not depend on anything—not on the environment, or an object, or a sensory organ. Consciousness is not something that I have or something that I can know—it is what I am, though in an impersonal way. In order to realize this, we need to free ourselves from the compulsion to know and consent to be.

To meditate in order to realize the nature of the mind is, in itself, simple, but it takes a lot of practice.

Mahamudra teacher Lama Genden Rinpoche instructs:

> In meditation, we simply allow our mind to rest in the present moment, to be present in the ungraspable now that is neither the past nor the future. This present moment cannot be grasped by the intellect. It is not an object of intellectual understanding and cannot be described. Trying to hint at it, we may say that it is the awareness of the direct experience of the present—beyond time and space.

Consciousness cannot be grasped. To take a realization of an unchanging nature of consciousness as the end of the spiritual path is a mistake for most Buddhist thinkers.

This pure presence, or pure knowing, as some people call it, this naked awareness held as existing, is the original confusion from which the illusory world of samsara is created.

a question of self

S AINT AUGUSTINE wondered:

> What is time? Who can explain simply and briefly?
>
> As long as no one asks me I know, but if someone asks me and I try to explain, I do not know.

Augustine is here concerned with time, but the same kind of inquiry can be applied to the self, for that matter, to any phenomenon.

In *The Myth of Sisyphus,* Albert Camus reflects on the nature of the self:

> For if I try to seize this self of which I feel sure, if I try to define and summarize it, it is nothing but water slipping through my fingers.
>
> I can sketch one by one all the aspects it is able to assume, all those likewise that have been attributed to it, this upbringing, this origin, this order or these silences, this nobility or this vileness. But aspects cannot be added up.
>
> This very heart which is mine will remain indefinable to me. Between the certainty I have of my existence and the content I try to give to that assurance, the gap will never be filled. Forever I shall be a stranger to myself.

In Buddhism, the self is not the only object under investigation. In fact, all phenomena are radically questioned. The notion of self receives much attention because it is at the root of much suffering. To claim that the self does not exist, while other phenomena really do, would be inconsistent.

However, for some Buddhist traditions, as for the master Mahasi Sayadaw, a few phenomena really exist. They are: space, nirvana, consciousness, mental factors, and the four elements (fire, earth, water, and air). Whereas for some thinkers of late Buddhism (Madhyamaka), when phenomena are questioned they cannot be said to exist or to not exist; they are just empty appearances.

There is a radical difference between the visions of the world before and after questioning.

At the superficial level of the everyday life before investigation, all phenomena are what they are. If I am not asked, I know.

But if I am asked . . .

There are two ways of questioning phenomena.

The first is a logical investigation. It is at at the level of knowledge, an objective inquiry even when it concerns the self. It seeks to know what is the reality of the phenomenon under investigation. It helps to loosen the certainty in the reality of the everyday world, but it is still bound by concept. Some traditions seem not to go beyond this kind of investigation.

The second way approaches the problem nonconceptually, either through a clear seeing of the chain of conditioning or from the side of awareness. The latter does not consider a particular phenomenon, but the role that intentionality plays in the presence of the objective and subjective worlds. It is not an investigation per se, but a withholding of intentionality through a rigorous meditation. Without intentionality there is no more language, thus it is no longer possible to deny or affirm anything. The mind, free of duality, does not pertain to knowing but to awareness. This is where we leave the world of logic and philosophy. We leave knowledge for wisdom.

What is behind the expressions "I" or "me"? Who is speaking when someone says "I"?

While Buddhism holds this question at its core, it is not unknown to other spiritual and philosophical traditions. However, the importance this question has in the Buddhist tradition differentiates it markedly from the others.

When other religions question the reality of the self they do not stop at the elusive nature of this perplexing entity—they quickly move on to something else.

In its quest for the the true self, Vedanta finds a consciousness, pure and eternal, and refers to it as *Atman*, or what the Anglo-Indian thinkers call "the Self" with a capital letter, so as to differentiate it from the limited self, which they also deem unreal.

Christian mystics and theologians have a particular way of seeing the "I."

> What I find deep inside myself is not me as "ego," but the Divine light.
>
> —Saint Augustine

> The word I does not belong to anyone other than to God—alone in his unity.
>
> —Meister Eckhart

Buddhism does not seek to replace the unreality of the self by something else, rather, it appreciates the space of freedom it offers.

MEDITATION THROUGH LOGICAL INVESTIGATION

When some wandering ascetics asked one of the master's main disciples, Anuradha, to know if the Buddha will exist after his death, he replied: "We cannot say that." So they asked him the opposite: Would he not exist after his death? He answered: "We cannot say that." The ascetics became upset. They insulted Anuradha and left. Perplexed, Anuradha went to seek counsel with the Buddha. Could it be that he had given them a wrong answer?

Before knowing whether someone will exist after his death, we should determine whether he exists now.

As they faced each other, the Buddha challenged Anuradha to find something that corresponds to the Buddha. Here, he used the term "Tathagatha" to speak of himself. He asked the monk whether the Tathagatha is one of his constituting aggregates, whether it is the body, the feeling tones, perception, volition, or consciousness. Is he the sum of the aggregates? Is he anything other than the aggregates? Anuradha could not put his finger on anything that is truly the Buddha. The Master concluded by affirming that it is useless to ask whether he will exist after his death if we cannot find what he is while alive.

This analysis will be repeatedly taken up by the majority of Buddhist traditions.

Why wouldn't a person be a collection of aggregates that constitute him or her? What would it mean to be constituted of various elements?

In an ancient text, this question is addressed by using the example of a wooden chariot obviously composed of various parts.

The story tells of a meeting in Punjab between a monk named Nagasena and a king of Greek origin named Milinda. The two men debate numerous questions, including the notion of the self.

The King approaches Nagasena and salutes him politely. The monk returns his greetings.

The King asks him his name.

"I go by the name of Nagasena: this is how my brothers call me. But, O King, while parents assign names to their children such as Surasena, Virasena, or Sihasena, it only an appellation, a simple name. It has no power over the individual."

Milinda then addresses the assembly: "Here is Nagasena, who claims that there is no individual under his name." Could we admit that?

Then, Nagasana explains: "O King, delicate as a prince. Does it happen that you walk barefoot in the mid-day sun on the hot ground, in the burning sand, treading the contours of gravel, shards and sand, your feet in suffering, your body weary, your soul exhausted? Have you come on foot or by means of a vehicle?"

King: I do not go on foot, O Venerable one, I came in a chariot.

Nagasana: Since you came in a chariot, Maharaja, tell me what is a chariot? Is it the tiller?

K: No, Venerable.

N: Is it the axle?

K: No, Venerable.

N: Is it the wheels, the cart, the yoke, the reigns, the spur?

K: No, Venerable.

N: Is it the sum of all those parts?

K: No, Venerable.

N: Is it a thing completely distinct from all this?

K: No, Venerable.

N: My interrogation is useless, I see no chariot. Maharaja, your word is false and misleading—there is no chariot.

The king tries to justify himself: "I am not lying, Venerable. It is from the tiller and the different parts that the common expression *chariot* is formed."

Then Nagasana explains to the king that it is on the basis of the different aggregates of the body and the consciousness that the appellation *Nagasena* is formed.

The Greeks used the story of the Ship of Theseus to illustrate how difficult it is to grasp the existence of a phenomenon constituted from a number of parts.

The ship on which Theseus embarked was a galley of thirty oars that the Athenians preserved for a very long time. When the time came, they replaced the worn-out and broken pieces of the ship by firmly attaching new ones to the remaining old. Philosophers cite this ship as an example illustrating doubt. Some believe that it is the same ship, while others argue that it is a different one.

Yet does the real Ship of Theseus not depend on conventions rather than in ways the old or the new pieces are assembled?

A monk asks the Buddha: "How is it that there is no "I" when each sutra begins with: "Thus have I heard?" The Buddha replies that the notion of "I" has three distinct sources: confusion, pride, and convention.

The first two should be given up and the third should be respected.

Not all thinkers have such measured opinions.

Pascal used to say that a respectable human being should not use the terms *I* and *me*.

ANOTHER TYPE OF MEDITATION

Another type of meditation shows that the human being is moved not by an independent entity—*I*—but by a chain of impersonal conditions. This chain is defined in the Suttas in the following way:

> When this exists, that comes to be.
> With the arising of this, that arises.
> When this does not exist, that does not come to be.
> With the cessation of this, that ceases.

This is not an affirmation of causality, but an observation of a succession of events. This chain does not describe the general aspects of things, but things at one particular moment. For example, the "body-mind" comes to signify the body and the mind at one particular moment, a moment that is a part of this chain. This sequence must be understood in the context of impermanence, where all phenomena change from one instant to another. Conditioned by ignorance, holding to the existence of a real and independent self, mental formations emerge. These mental formations are psychological conditionings such as arrogance, pride, and anxiety. They all lead to certain types

of behavior at particular moments. Conditioned by these mental for-
mations, consciousness appears; a particular type of consciousness at
each moment, such as for example, a worried consciousness. Condi-
tioned by the consciousness, the body-mind arises; conditioned by the
body-mind, the sense organs; conditioned by the sense organs, contact.
Contact that means a felt experience, is that moment of consciousness
when an object, a sense organ, and attention meet. Conditioned by felt
experience, feeling arises; from feeling, desire (or another type of emo-
tion); from desire, clinging; from clinging, becoming; from becoming,
birth; from birth, old age, sickness, and death.

The confusion arises from the identification with any of these ele-
ments. When ignorance attached to the reality of the self ceases, the
chain of conditioning does so as well.

Nietzsche noted:

> One thinks; but that this "one" is precisely the famous old
> "ego," is, to put it mildly, only a supposition, an assertion, and
> assuredly not an "immediate certainty."

Ignorance is not a simple lack of knowledge, but imagination. It
projects the concept "I" onto the various links of the chain. Medita-
tive presence frees from this confusion, leaving thought and desire to
themselves. When the *I* is no more, the chain stops.

The self, for Buddhism, is only a conventional designation, a repre-
sentation. Confusion mistakes I for a real, autonomous, and indepen-
dent entity. However, and thanks to contemporary psychology, we must
admit that this representation plays an important role in the develop-
ment and the functioning of human beings.

Eirich Neuman, Jung's disciple, describes the emergence of (self-)
consciousness:

> The history of human consciousness was the gradual extrac-
> tion of a small but a growing and increasingly clear and

self-determined focus on inner human experience from a dream-like state of virtual identity with body and environment.

Elsewhere he writes:

Just as the infantile ego, living this phase over again, feebly developed, easily tired, emerges like an island out of the ocean of the unconscious for occasional moment only, and sinks back again, so early man experiences the world.

It is precisely the notion of "I/me" that allows this island of consciousness to emerge, to extract itself from the oceanic depths.

Let us imagine how the sense of "I" develops from early childhood.

This sense is not innate, but is transmitted from the mother to the newborn child. For psychoanalysts, an infant at the early stages of life does not distinguish itself from its mother or its environment. It is not conscious of itself, but is merged with the world that surrounds it. We could imagine the state of wholeness preceding the separation of the subject from the object, a state of confusion without a clear self-consciousness.

As Winnicott points out, at the beginning the infant is the surrounding and the surrounding is the infant.

The mother's projective identification[*] is certainly essential in the infant's construction of the sense of self. But, the mother transmits not only this sense of self, but also a boundless love toward this self. Such love is certainly necessary to gather the energy needed for the considerable task that an infant undertakes.

Self-consciousness, more subtle than consciousness of objects, is a

---

[*] Projective identification is the projection of parts of the self into an object (a person). The object is perceived as having acquired the characteristics of the projected part of the self, but in the self may also become identified with the object of its projection.

sign of a greater maturity. At first, access to self-consciousness necessitates a release from the initial sate of fusion and the capacity to distinguish oneself from others. As described before, consciousness can function as a subjective center only by creating a representation of itself, a representation that seems to exist at the level of objects. "I" is something other than self-consciousness. However, the tendency to confuse *I* and consciousness is persistent.

The third Karmapa's "Aspirational Prayer for Mahamudra" says,

> Under the power of ignorance, we mistake self-consciousness
> for an *I*.

And Freud, in his correspondence with Romain Rolland, said, with a certain reserve, that he could not conceive of the mystical experience except as a regression to the oceanic state of infancy. But Freud would lend his ear to neurotics only, not to mystics.

There is a deep confusion here, a confusion that Ken Wilbert calls "the pre/trans fallacy."

It is important to differentiate between the two stages of human development in which consciousness is not enclosed by the notion of *I*. One of these two states of nondual (non-differentiated) consciousness precedes the development of the *I;* the other follows and transcends it. Without this important distinction, the inner experiences of the greatest philosophers and mystics can only be understood in terms of regression.

From the few remarks made earlier about consciousness, the pre-egoïc stage can be defined as a fusion between consciousness and objects: consciousness takes itself to be what it perceives, what it feels. At the trans-egoïc stage, consciousness is, above all, conscious of itself through each experience. It is pure presence. The first stage is a state of extreme confusion, inhibiting all human behavior, making it difficult to relate to the everyday world. At the second stage, consciousness is capable of dealing with the world in a more lucid and efficient way than at the egoïc-stage.

Another very frequent mistake is to take pathological states for mystical experiences. These few lines below, taken from Nijinsky's diary, illustrate the use of mystical language by a disturbed person.

> I can do everything. I am a servant. I am a factory worker. I am a gentleman. I am an aristocrat. I am a Tzar. I am an emperor. I am God. I am God. I am God. I am everything. I am life. I am eternity. I will be always and everywhere. People will kill me but I will live because I am everything.

These two nondual states have in common the fact that they are not enclosed within the limits of *I*. Other than that, they have nothing in common.

Nonetheless, the *I* is a notion that is essential for the development of self-consciousness and its maturation. Any disturbance in this development can lead to serious difficulties.

Ronald Laing cites a case of a patient who lacks a stable notion of his reality:

> I forgot myself at the Ice Carnival the other night. I was so absorbed in looking at it that I forgot what time it was and who and where I was. When I suddenly realized I hadn't been thinking about myself I was frightened to death. The unreality feeling came. I must never forget myself for a single minute.

The questioning of the sense of self does not precipitate mentally balanced individuals into confusion regarding their own reality. On the contrary, the state of pure presence that can develop in meditation is experienced with a total sense of evidence, but as we will see, meditation does not stop here.

The sense of existing cannot be reduced to the sense of self. Personalization of presence gives it an appearance of consistency, but of confinement as well.

The self manifests in two contradictory aspects. On the one hand, it is stable and seems to endure. On the other hand, it constantly manifests under different aspects.

I am certain of being the same person throughout my life, whether it is at the age of five, or twenty, or fifty, yet I have changed physically, emotionally, intellectually, and socially. What is common in these different instances of me? There must be something similar in these instances to have this impression of consistency. The similarity cannot be found in the shape of the body, or social status, or in psychological maturity. The only element that remains constant throughout a lifetime is self-awareness in each experience, as described above. The unity of consciousness does not depend on a self, but on this self-awareness.

Knowledge grasps this phenomenon, emerging at every moment like itself, by the concept *I* and generates a feeling of permanence. *I* is mainly a representation of self-awareness, its personification. It is akin to a thing, not to a consciousness.

· *I* is not an abstract word like, for example, *contrarily*. It has a way of appearing that commonly relies on the speaker's body image. When the appearance of our body is damaged by old age, for example, we suffer. But it would be wrong to say that the *I* has deteriorated. Suffering, in this case, results essentially from pride affected by the deterioration of the body's image.

There is also another, more general way for the self to appear—a way that includes body-mind as a whole.

To illustrate this, a Tibetan master gives the following example: Imagine that someone pricks you with a needle. You jump. What is affected here is not only the body, but an *I* that combines body and mind. If someone accuses you of a wrongdoing that you haven't committed, this offended self cannot be reduced either to the body or to the mind, but it encompasses both.

Consciousness has no objective characteristics through which it can be apprehended. Its representative—*I*—uses aspects of the present experience to take on an appearance that is either physical, "I am tall,"

"I am stooped," and so forth, or spiritual, "I am intelligent," "I am sad," and so on, or both, "I am home."

It is because the "I" does not possess its own characteristics, as with the words "here" and "there," that it can take on so many different aspects.

This limited aspect of the "I" makes it vulnerable and incomplete, and thus is endlessly under the sway of worry and desire, but those emotions do not affect self-consciousness, which is necessarily impersonal.

Because self-consciousness is free from limitations, from duality, it is a totality and thus cannot be prey to attachment or to desire. Who would desire, and what would be its object?

At the level of consciousness, death carries no meaning. It cannot imagine its own passing away, as it would need to be present to experience it.

Death has a meaning only for the self.

Freud calls nirvana a drive that seeks to attain a state of no-tension. For him it is a death-drive. However, he can only conceive of this tensionlessness as a return to an archaic state. He does not move beyond the point of view of the *I*.

Suffering and the end of suffering are the main subjects of the Buddha's teachings. He teaches the ending of birth, old age, sickness, and death, here and now. But the master might seem to have given a bad example by attaining the advanced age of 80, getting seriously ill, and dying.

It is obvious that Buddhism does not aspire to immortality.

Through identification and, therefore, thingification, consciousness takes up a fate similar to that of things and to that of the body in particular. By taking itself for a corporeal "I," consciousness grows old, withers, crumbles, and prepares to die. But this is only the body's destiny. To say that the self is not the body does not mean that it is outside of it. This would entail a rather unwise disassociation. The "I" cannot be grasped in such and such way because it is only a conventional designation, a grammatical particle, as Nietzsche states.

If we consider someone to be nice, where is this "niceness" located? It would be useless to look for it in the person—it is not there. Moreover, it is probable that this point of view is not unanimous. It is not because we all use the terms *I* or *you* almost unanimously, that they can be located. They cannot be pinpointed any more than the concept "nice" or words like "here" and "there."

MEDITATION BASED ON AWARENESS

An attentive presence, bereft of intention, as it is cultivated in meditation, unveils a consciousness devoid of self, of the duality of subject and object, and finally is free of grasping.

The Bahiya Sutta makes the point clearly:

Bahiya, who had doubts about his practice, pressured the Buddha to give him concise instructions for the practice of meditation. The Buddha advised him to meditate in such a way that while seeing there would be only seeing, while hearing there would be only hearing, while tasting there would be only tasting, while smelling there would be only smelling, while feeling a physical sensation there would be only sensing, and while thinking there would be only thinking. The Buddha concluded: "Then you will be neither here nor there (neither in the object nor the subject), nor in-between—this is the end of suffering, this is nirvana."

This same principle applies to all emotions.

It is really a question of being the experience; of being intimate with hearing, with sadness or joy for example, so as to realize their fundamentally impersonal nature. In such closeness, such intimacy, there is no place for "I." There is only a sad, happy, or bored consciousness. It is not so much a question of recognizing and naming the emotion, but of living it. Joy is present to itself; it does need "I" to experience it.

It is not a matter of being conscious only of the physical symptoms of emotions, like heaviness on the chest, but of accurately perceiving the quality of consciousness that is sadness, for example. It is only then that it can be experienced in an impersonal and serene way.

According to some masters, we should be careful not to create an abstract voidness.

When we decompose a compound, it is clear that the compound no longer exists.

When we are left with parts lying on the ground after having pulled apart a chariot, then to realize that there is no chariot anymore is not a realization of its emptiness.

It would be quite strange that, to investigate the real nature of something, we must get rid of that thing altogether. That would imply a negation of the world.

The emptiness of a phenomenon is not realized by getting rid of its presence, but by seeing it with a nondual mind, a nongrasping mind, which realizes the inseparability of appearance and emptiness.

To deconstruct a person into its various constituents and to discover that there is no longer a human being is not a realization of the person's emptiness. It is simply an abstract game: a game that can be instructive at times, but does not lead us to see reality.

"I" and "you," just like "here" and "there," are expressions devoid of essence, but not of meaning. This realization does not prevent dialogue: on the contrary, it brings lightness to it.

At the closing of these meditations, "I" has not been destroyed because it never really existed. Only the illusion of its reality has been dispelled.

unconditioned

H ow does the world appear to a sage according to Buddhism? It could be interesting to describe what distinguishes the Buddhist vision from other spiritual traditions, not necessarily to show Buddhism's superiority, but to underline what characterizes it.

Trying to convince ourselves that all traditions lead to the same goal is a superficial way of approaching the problem. It might be an excuse to not deepen the question.

Almost all religions believe in a unique source of existence. For some it is God, for others it is the One, Pure Consciousness, or the Brahman.

WHAT REALLY EXISTS FOR BUDDHISM?

Language is powerless to describe a vision that lies beyond concepts. The language used by mystics and yogis is necessarily ambiguous and can be applied to similar but radically different experiences.

Only theology or philosophy that the mystic advocates, or its tradition, permits an understanding of its deep meaning.

Buddhist thinkers have extensively debated with the followers of other Indian traditions, such as Advaita (nonduality), on the subject of reality. They have agreed on one thing: their points of view are divergent.

For Hindu thinkers, Buddhists go too far in their negation—they are nihilists. For Buddhists, the Hindus do not go far enough—they are not free from grasping, and, therefore, from illusion.

Advaita relates everything to consciousness. Everything is being, consciousness, and bliss.

One of the most ancient Vedic texts—the Rig Veda—affirms that:"Mind has neither origination nor destruction, nor even stability."

Some Buddhist texts also seem to be attached to an absolute. Sometimes, they even reintroduce the notion of the Self. Their point of view seems close to Advaita. This causes some tensions within the Buddhist tradition. Dogen, the founder of Japanese Soto Zen, for example, castigates the monks who think that:

> If you really understand that the mind nature existing in our body is not subject to birth and death, then since it is the original nature, although the body is only a temporary form haphazardly born here and dying, the mind is permanent and unchangeable in the past, present, and future. To know this is called release from life and death.

Faithful to the primitive doctrine of the Buddha, most Buddhist thinkers do not believe in an absolute, immovable, and eternal reality, and, even more radically, they do not consider a Self as this absolute. The Buddha constantly sets himself apart from the Hindu tradition, and his objections to their doctrine remain valid even with respect to the later developments of the Vedic tradition, like those of the Advaita.

Some quotations could fit into texts belonging either to one, or the other traditions, giving the impression that there are no differences between them. But we must not forget that they emanate from different visions of the world.

Consider this from Richard King's *Early Advaita and Buddhism*:

> There is neither cessation nor origination; no one in bondage, no one aspiring, no one desirous of liberation, no one who is emancipated. This is the highest truth.

This quotation from a text of the Advaita literature is consistent with its vision that only the Brahman, the One, the Absolute Being is real. Arising and vanishing phenomena are mere illusion.

They are but the dream or the Maya (magic) of Vishnu, according to certain Hindu sects.

Some Christian mystics, such as Meister Eckhart, teach that the creation is a pure nothing because it receives its being from another, from God.

For Madhyamaka, everything existing depends on other things; nothing has true, independent existence; nothing really arises, nothing really ceases. Finally there is nothing to grasp, there is no absolute. Vishnu and his Maya no more exist than any other phenomenon.

Nonduality for Buddhism is not the nonduality of the Atman and the Brahman, as for some Hindu systems, nor merely of subject and object, but, more radically, between being and non-being.

From the Kaccayana Sutta

> The Venerable Kaccayana Gotta approached the Blessed One and, on arrival, having bowed down, sat to one side. As he was sitting there he said to the Blessed One: "Lord, 'Right view, right view,' it is said. To what extent is there right view?"
>
> "By and large, Kaccayana, this world is supported by the polarity of existence and non-existence. But when one sees the origination of the world as it actually is with right discernment, 'non-existence' with reference to the world does not occur to one. When one sees the cessation of the world as it actually is with right discernment, 'existence' with reference to the world does not occur to one.
>
> "'Everything exists': That is one extreme. 'Everything doesn't exist': That is a second extreme. Avoiding these two extremes, the Tathagata teaches the Dhamma via the middle."

To affirm nonexistence by pretending that all is emptiness is a mistake that Hindu thinkers often attribute to Buddhism.

The Heart Sutra is often evoked to express the Buddhist vision of the world. But it clearly states:

> Form is emptiness, emptiness is form.
> Form is no other than emptiness, emptiness is no other than form.

Consciousness is not more real than other phenomena:

> Consciousness is emptiness; emptiness is consciousness.
> Consciousness is no other than emptiness; emptiness is no other than consciousness.

To take only a part of the statement and to pretend that everything is emptiness, or that consciousness is emptiness, is misleading.

We would rather like to follow the Buddhist thinkers who teach that to meditate on emptiness while getting rid of appearances is a negation of the world. To realize the true mode of being of the world, its suchness, it is to realize the inseparability of appearances and emptiness.

The Sakyapa Masters express that clearly: appearance is established as empty; emptiness is affirmed as dependent origination; emptiness and appearance are inseparable; and this unity cannot be expressed by words.

It is beyond any view.

Buddhism avoids the two extremes of idealism and materialism. Perhaps it succeeds in reconciling matter and mind by refusing to take sides. Because neither one really exists, they can interact. Thought confines them in concepts that set them apart, then it wonders why it is so difficult to bring them together.

In the Buddhist tradition, the question of being is approached from the angle of causality and interdependence. Refusing to set an absolute at the foundation of everything, Buddhism questions the nature of phenomena and of the *I*.

The Dalai Lama quotes Nagarjuna as follows:

> If there existed somewhere a being unborn, this being could come into being, but since such a being does not exist, what could come into being?

In other words, if something exists it does not need to be born, if something does not exist how can we speak of its birth?

The notions of being and of non-being are both dead ends.

Questioning in the Buddhist tradition evolves, going from the self to consciousness, or from the self to phenomena. Ultimately, the analysis concerns the human experience in its entirety: consciousness—body—world.

The gradual approach, first focusing the mind on the clear and knowing aspect of consciousness then realizing its emptiness, and, finally, recognizing the indivisibility of appearance and emptiness, is described with precision in numerous Buddhist texts.

But there is also a sudden way, which is taught by some traditions and which leaves no concessions for concepts of a path or of a goal.

This does not mean that some preparations are not needed.

When you want to sleep, you set the proper condition: you put on light clothing, you turn off the radio and the TV set, you lie down and turn off the light. That does not cause the sleep, but it makes it possible.

One comes to a point where one stops doing anything, even wanting to sleep.

Questioning is limited to the level of knowledge. Indeed, for knowledge, something either exists or it does not; it cannot move beyond this duality. But this impossibility is specific to knowledge, not to awareness.

According to Buddhism, it is not reality that confines humans within samsara, but points of view.

Madhyamaka, certainly the most original Buddhist school of thought, offers no theory: it is a style, a radical questioning that denies nothing and affirms nothing. It is an invitation to move in the world, free from grasping.

This is clearly mentioned in the Duttatthaka Sutta:

> One who is attached argues over doctrines—How and with what does one argue with someone unattached?
>
> Embracing nothing, rejecting nothing, right here, a person has shaken off every view.

The Madhyamaka tries to use a language that does not give anything to grasp.

And the Vimalakirti Sutra says:

> Reverend Sariputra, he who is interested in the Dharma is not interested in recognizing suffering, abandoning its origination, realizing its cessation, or practicing the path. Why? The Dharma is ultimately without formulation and without verbalization. He who verbalizes: 'Suffering should be recognized, origination should be eliminated, cessation should be realized, the path should be practiced,' is not interested in the Dharma but is interested in verbalization.

Sometimes silence seems more eloquent:

> Then the crown prince Manjushri said to the Licchavi Vimalakirti, "We have all given our own teachings, noble sir. Now, may you elucidate the teaching of the entrance into the principle of nonduality!"
>
> Thereupon, the Licchavi Vimalakirti kept his silence, saying nothing at all.

He refuses to reduce wisdom to concepts. Exiled into the world of knowledge and language, wisdom is stammering, clumsy.

"The Albatross," by Baudelaire, illustrates such a fall:

> Often, to amuse themselves, the men of a crew
> Catch albatrosses, those vast sea birds
> That indolently follow a ship
> As it glides over the deep, briny sea.
> Scarcely have they placed them on the deck
> Than these kings of the sky, clumsy, ashamed,
> Pathetically let their great white wings
> Drag beside them like oars.
> That winged voyager, how weak and gauche he is,
> So beautiful before, now comic and ugly!
> One man worries his beak with a stubby clay pipe;
> Another limps, mimics the cripple who once flew!
> The poet resembles this prince of cloud and sky
> Who frequents the tempest and laughs at the bowman;
> When exiled on the earth, the butt of hoots and jeers,
> His giant wings prevent him from walking.

The most sacred notions of Buddhism are no more real than any other phenomena. Vimalakirti asserts this point in a provocative way.

To force his audience to free themselves from the belief in the reality of "right" and "wrong," Vimalakirti preaches the practice of the "wrong":

> Then, the crown prince Manjushri said to the Licchavi Vimalakirti, "Noble sir, how does the bodhisattva follow the way to attain the qualities of the Buddha?"
>
> Vimalakirti replied, "Manjushri, when the bodhisattva follows the wrong way, he follows the way to attain the qualities of the Buddha."

To believe that there is a right and a wrong path is to take the dead-ends of being and nonbeing.

When we oppose samsara to nirvana it is impossible to move from one to another. If samsara and nirvana were to really exist, it would be impossible to free ourselves from samsara.

Between samsara and nirvana lies an uncrossable abyss. It cannot be crossed because it has always already been crossed.

The belief that samsara and nirvana really exist creates the abyss, and the desire to cross it makes it uncrossable.

To understand this, not to mention realizing it, for most of us, requires a lot of practice.

This is not a belief, but a vision. Those who, not seeing it, would make it a truth, are desperately lost. This vision is completely ordinary, but it does not grasp anything as existing or nonexisting.

Lin-chi, the great Ch'an master, expresses this vision very simply:

> As I see it, there isn't so much to do. Just be ordinary—put on your clothes, eat your food, and pass the time doing nothing. You who come here from here and there all have a mind to seek buddha, to seek dharma, to seek emancipation, to seek escape from the three realms. Foolish fellows! When you've left the three realms where would you go?

A Zen parable puts it this way:

> A monk told Joshu: "I have just entered your monastery. Please teach me."
> Joshu asked: "Have you eaten your rice porridge?"
> The monk replied: "I have."
> Joshu said: "Then you wash your bowl."
> At that moment the monk was enlightened.

responsibility and engagement

Once everything has been relinquished so thoroughly, how can any concern for the world still be justified?

Buddhism does so through compassion.

Doesn't Vimalakirti's teaching affirm that compassion without wisdom is bondage? Likewise, wisdom without compassion is bondage.

Here, the term "compassion" includes all virtues such as kindness, generosity, patience, and so on, except for wisdom.

The power of thought can lead to either a deeper state of servitude or greater freedom.

To develop virtue, thought must be used wisely.

Dostoevsky wrote: "In a world without God, everything is permitted." But isn't it a little too quickly said? It is an affirmation that can only be that of a believer. When a superior being sanctions human actions, responsibility is reduced to accepting the punishment, as with a thief for whom the only problem is getting caught, rather than the pain inflicted on a victim, or like a driver who, parking his car in a red zone, doesn't care about the flow of traffic or the safety of pedestrians, but about the ticket.

It is risky to make morality dependent on faith in God. When this faith disappears, man wanders in a meaningless world.

Without a superior being to preside over retributions, I must take the responsibility for both my acts and their consequences. I cannot cancel it by serving some penalty. There is no tribunal to call upon—I remain with my responsibility; it cannot be shared.

This morality without retribution, but not without consequence, confronts us with the most urgent demand.

Responsibility requires the possibility of choice. Vice, the slave of passions, allows no freedom to choose: it possesses the mind it inhabits.

Wisdom, on the other hand, choosing always the way of freedom, can only opt for virtue. When virtue does not depend on any calculations, evading social ostracism or divine punishment, when it is authentic, it does not force—it sets free.

How could there be freedom in avoidance and dissimulation, in the refusal to take responsibility for one's own existence? How can we be free without consenting to be present?

With different tenses, responsibility takes on different meanings: to take responsibility for one's actions performed in the past, to fully be in the present, and to engage with and commit to the future.

Responsibility cannot be reduced to the willingness to take responsibility for one's past actions. It is much more significant as an ability to engage, to promise.

In the Buddhist tradition, the commitment to take care of others is called the "mind of awakening."

Every day, followers of Zen, of Tibetan Buddhism, and of other traditions take the vow to free all beings from suffering.

From the beginning of the spiritual path, these vows help to deepen the meaning of this responsibility.

I cannot leave to someone else the responsibility to take care of others. In such endeavors "I am irreplaceable," taught Shantideva.

The mind of awakening has two aspects: intention and action.

Simone Weil asserts that the distinction between justice and generosity was invented to excuse the fortunate from helping the poor. We might excuse ourselves from being generous and tolerant but it is hard to excuse ourselves from being just. I could naïvely imagine that my miserliness or lack of compassion affects only those to whom I close my heart, but I clearly see my injustice.

> *Nobody can violate the integrity of another being but by losing his own.*
>
> —Bossuet

When generosity is seen as a matter of justice, it is no longer easy to walk past a beggar on the sidewalk. I can accept not being generous, but can I accept being unjust?

Perhaps we should extend this idea to other virtues like compassion, kindness, sympathy, and morality. Then, egoism, greed, or malevolence, would be forms of injustice.

If we follow Simone Weil's argument, charity does not depend on reason, but on seeing others in their humanity—that is enough.

Shantideva says,

> Those desiring
> To protect themselves and others quickly
> Should practice the supreme mystery
> Switching "self" and "other."

To see the other in his humanity, we must first challenge the legitimacy of the central position to which the self feels entitled.

In fact, I am I only for me: for all the others, and they are numerous, I am another. It is very unlikely that they are all wrong.

> *What is this I that is I for me and a not-I for all the others?*
> —*Aryadeva*

What would it mean to be another? It would not be a mater of trading the confinement of my particularities for someone else's, but of discovering what all people have in common.

THE FIRST STEP

To meditate on this is the first step toward altruism.

I imagine myself walking on a busy street in a big city. I see innumerable crowds of people: here's a person, and another one, and another. It is endless. But I am also one person among the others—perfectly replaceable. If I imagine myself going through the doors of a coffee shop, to the waiter I am just another customer. When I walk into the subway, for those already there I am only another traveler.

In meditation, we must consider many such situations and realize what it means to be another person, while avoiding the trap of mere self-observation like, for example, observing oneself walk, or hearing oneself talk. It is not about distancing from oneself or projecting oneself into the gaze of the other. We should never leave our own place. But little by little, through practice, it becomes clear what "being another" means.

Then it is wise to consider difficulties—suffering, disease, and even death—from this point of view. Then one's own death is not a special burden, as so many others die each day. The fact that this "other" that I am encounters difficulties, as so many others do, is no longer devastating. It becomes clear that egoism, rather than a pleasant indulgence, is an intolerable pressure. To consider oneself as another drains away the disproportionate importance that we attribute to ourselves and allows the development of real kindness toward self and others.

Up until now, presence has been considered on its own, relying solely on itself. But it is also important in relationship to others. Here, the problem shifts: it is no longer the objectification of my own emotions or my states of consciousness—but the reduction of the other to the status of a thing, an object of desire, of worry, or of anger. This confusion is always two-fold: if I objectify the other, I lose my own humanity. Then there is no place for altruism or any other virtue, because there are no more people. A solidarity amongst things is meaningless.

Shantirakshita tells us:

> Consciousness arises as the contrary of matter, gross, inani-
> mate. By nature, mind is immaterial and it is self-aware.

This self-consciousness is particular to human beings.

When a person identifies with a profession or an activity, he gives himself the consistency of an object and loses his humanity. In our humanity we are united in sameness; in identification we are diverse and separate. To approach the other in the guise of a man or a woman, a straight or gay, a physician, a social worker, or a plumber sets us apart.

RECOGNITION OF THE OTHER

Shantideva declares:

> Therefore I'll dispel the pain of others,
> For it is pain, just like my own.
> And I will take care of others
> For they are living beings, like myself.

But this recognition is difficult. In Indian Buddhism, and also in the Tibetan tradition, spiritual exercises are taught to overcome this difficulty.

Some texts recommend seeing all beings as a mother sees her child, other texts as a friend, and still others like one's own mother. As all beings are moved by similar attitudes, Shantideva recommends to see them as oneself.

> What happiness is for me, it is for others
> What suffering is for me, it is for others

If a person cuts in line at the bakery to get to the last loaf of bread, it is not because she hates me, but she loves that bread as much as I do.

If a driver steals my parking spot, it is not because he wants to harm me on purpose, but because, just like me, he simply doesn't want to spend time searching for another spot. Understanding this person's motivation helps me recognize how similar we are.

Simone Weil puts this in a nutshell:

> To recognize that this hungry person, is a human being like myself is enough. The rest follows by itself.

The egoist strips the other of this humanity by placing him on the side of things. This is one of the most serious of injustices. Even judges sometimes commit the injustice of reducing the condemned to an offense, thus locking him into a cycle of delinquency. How can the sense of justice be restored in the mind of a prisoner if his dignity has been stripped away?

Weil:

> He who treats as equals those who are far below him in strength really makes them a gift of the quality of human beings, of which fate had deprived them.

For this, it is important to become conscious of the way the others are reduced to the state of mere things—how they become invisible.

Patrick Declerk, a psychiatrist who spent some time with people living on the streets of Paris, describes his experience of begging in the Metro:

> Whatever the technique, you must face insults and disdainful looks. In order to continue to exist in front of those who look away, it is necessary to fight against the insidious feeling of having become invisible.

It is not so much poverty itself that is deplorable but the banishment of the beggar from society which treats him as a penniless good-for-nothing.

Categorizing is a means of placing the other out of the human sphere. This artifice is used to frightening effect in genocides. To confine a person to the category of "foreigner," or "Jew," "infidel," "homosexual,"or "drunk" objectifies the person, separates him, casts him out.

But this exclusion is sometimes generated by the afflicted himself, as if, in order not to feel the weight of his affliction, he places himself on the outskirts of society—of a society that does not make the same demands of outcasts.

Few philosophers have such a deep knowledge of human suffering as Simone Weil:

> Affliction is anonymous before all things: it deprives its victims of their personality and make them into things. It is indifferent.
>
> Another effect of affliction is little by little, to make the soul its accomplice, by injecting a poison of inertia into it. In anyone who has suffered affliction for a long time there is complicity with regard to his own affliction.

To take a superior position means that we are enforcing a solidification, an objectification of ourselves and of the other, thus falling from our own humanity. There can be no value difference between two "humanities."

Once, on a very hot summer day in New York, I walked into a café. While I was looking for an empty table, I noticed a man dressed in a heavy woolen coat. There was a free table next to his and I chose to sit there. While unhurriedly drinking my iced coffee, I observed. His hands were protected by plastic gloves. A black notebook was on the table. He was writing, but "doodling" would describe his activity better. He was filling up pages and turning them with a sharp gesture. At this pace, his notebook was going to be filled soon. At that very moment, a couple walked in: the man and the woman both had white hair and were wearing the same sky-blue shorts, the same sneakers, and the same white polo shirts. They found a table near the man with the woolen coat. Because a chair was missing at their table, the man who had just arrived took one from the table of the man in the coat. From the conversation that the couple had with a young customer sitting at a table next to them, I learned that they had come from San Francisco to spend a few days of vacation in New York.

When they had finished their coffees, the man got up and replaced the chair he had taken. On his way out, he patted the shoulder of the doodler, who was still working away and said, "Good work, good work, go on!" The doodler emitted a kind of grunt of satisfaction. I was stupefied. How could this man, this tourist, reach through to this strange artist over an abyss that seemed unbridgeable? He had given him back his humanity.

The practice of generosity often allows for the deepest humane encounters. It is, essentially, the letting go of attachment, even though it is motivated by kindness. Nobody can be fooled: giving away something that you no longer want is not an act of generosity.

Perhaps this encounter can be due to the uncompelled nature of the act, which implies the freedom of both the giver and the receiver. Of course, this is very different from having to fulfill your obligation to the shopowner by paying for something you pick up at a shop.

Generosity loses its grandeur when the giver expects something in return, such as an accumulation of merit or the assurance that God will recompense 100-fold. Then, the beggar is reduced to a pretext for the essentially selfish act, and it is quite possible that he feels it as such.

There is also a difference in status among beggars. Some beg for themselves, some belong to organized groups, and some are street musicians. Generally, the contact is different in each case. Those who belong to a group do not receive fully; it is the group that receives. They are unavailable for contact, as they are always already looking for

REFLECTIONS IN ESSAY   225

another good soul. Street musicians place an intermediary between themselves and the giver: the music. They lack the vulnerability of those who beg for themselves, with nothing to share but their suffering. These are truly vulnerable because, for them, there is nowhere to hide. This vulnerability exposes their humanity.

The act of generosity can become an occasion for a real meeting and the recognition of a common humanity. Sometimes, the drunken state of the homeless is too advanced for such an encounter to take place.

I remember a beautiful summer morning in the city of Avignon. As I was walking on the sidewalk, I encountered two homeless people who were already a little bit drunk. I stopped. As I gave them some change, my eyes met their gaze. Suddenly the men were completely here, present for this unique encounter. I felt fully existing.

Thus Buber asserts that a total act is an encounter through which the other is affirmed and known in the totality of his being.

To recognize the humanity of the other is essential. However, we must not forget each person's particularity. A rabbi from the Hassidic tradition taught that at the birth of each person something new is placed in the world, something that has never existed before—an original and unique thing.

Compassion is the care for the suffering of others. It is the opposite of indifference. Here, the use of the term "pity" seems unwise because it implies a feeling of superiority on the part of the one who feels it.

For compassion to arise there must be a suffering being. A happy person cannot be the subject of compassion, nor can an old wardrobe, nor an old table or a chair. When, for one reason or another, a suffering person is objectified and his suffering is rejected, compassion cannot be awakened.

To reduce a suffering person to the status of a thing is a very common attitude. Too often an ailing person suffers from exclusion, a prisoner of his handicap. This exclusionary attitude may come not only from the physician, but also from family and friends, as if the patient has crossed a line and left the world of those who are well. He is on the other side now, suddenly a pariah. Simone Weil notes that, in misery, all innocents feel damned.

It is important to see a person as a complete being, even if she suffers from a handicap. But any suffering can create the sense of being diminished. For a person on welfare, for example, the feeling of exclusion may be just as painful as the material difficulties he confronts.

Some people do not want to face suffering. When they come to the scene of an accident, for example, they avert their gaze. While visiting a friend at the hospital, they may try to avoid her. They can keep themselves busy by changing the water in the flower vase, or by going to get a bottle of water. If someone is bedridden after an accident, one way of avoiding the encounter is to talk about the circumstances, or by making statements like, "If only you hadn't taken the car that day." Thus they deny the suffering, rather than looking the person in the eye and recognizing it.

For compassion to awaken, a certain willingness to be with a person and her pain is necessary. We could also add the ability to put ourselves in the place of the other without losing ourselves, and serenely enduring her suffering, showing her that she is not excluded and that her pain is bearable.

In *Words That Touch*, the Genevan psychoanalyst Danielle Quinodoz describes an essential aspect of her work, which to a large extent echoes the Tibetan practice of taking the pain of another and giving them one's own happiness. She explains that, during analysis, patients often project their suffering and difficulties onto her. She must find within herself the strength to feel these difficulties without getting submerged, and then to reflect them back in a way that the patient can receive.

In psychology, to project a part of oneself onto the other is called "projective identification." It is a means of protecting oneself or part of oneself, but also of exercising control over the other.

Anna Freud describes a case of a young woman who liked to dress up and go out dancing. One day, a young man to whom she was attracted rang her doorbell. But it was her sister that he asked out. From this moment on, the young woman stopped caring about the clothes she was wearing, and no longer felt any pleasure from dancing. She adopted an attitude that could be mistaken for altruism. She got involved in the organization of her friends' weddings and lost herself completely in their happiness. She projected a part of herself onto her friends, a part that was lost to her.

Not all expressions of altruism are genuine. Sometimes they can lose their authenticity to exaggeration.

For Buddhism, equanimity plays an important part in the development of altruism. It introduces an element of wisdom that prevents the self-defeating excesses of kindness, compassion, and sympathy.

The object of kindness is the happiness of others, and generosity is one of its main manifestations. Compassion is the concern for those in pain and difficulty. Sympathy is the rejoicing in the well-being of the other.

As well as impartiality, equanimity carries a sense of being aware that the destiny of the other belongs to him and that I cannot impose my wishes upon him. Equanimity protects both me and others from having my kindness or compassion perverted into a means of exercising power.

The most important aspect of compassion practice is equanimity, the ability to remain open to one's own suffering and to that of others. Contrary to what Nietzsche sometimes proclaimed, compassion is not a sign of weakness but of courage. Far from being a burden, it is, above all, serenity, freedom from worry, disgust, and confusion.

In his quest for a balanced relationship with others, Shantideva suggests a way to free oneself from pride and envy.

He uses passion itself to free oneself from passion.

> Take others—lower, higher, equal—as yourself.
>   Identify yourself as "other,"
>   Then, without another thought, immerse yourself in envy,
> pride, and rivalry.

He's the center of attention. I am nothing.
And, unlike him, I'm poor, without possessions.
Everyone looks up to him, despising me,
All goes well for him; for me there's only bitterness!

Tibetan commentators have further refined this approach.

They suggested introducing a third person, someone hypothetical who has nothing to do with the situation.

If I experience pride with respect to a certain person, then I should place myself in a position where I become the object of disdain, a position from which I would suffer the pride of others. So I imagine a person who could treat me with contempt and another person for whom I could feel contempt. This creates a triad. I imagine what a contemptuous person could say about me. "Who does he think he is? Really, he's just pathetic, and so on." Don't hold back here. Then, I reflect on the way I see the person who seems inferior to me, the one toward whom I feel contempt. Suddenly I understand that my attitude is no longer credible. This method is infallible.

To neutralize envy, I proceed in a similar way. I create a new triad. I imagine a person who could have reasons to be envious of me, and I put myself in her place to adopt her point of view: "Why is it always he who gets invited, who gets introduced, who gets praised, what has he got that's so special, and so on." Then I return to myself and imagine the person of whom I'm envious. These same comments, which seemed so charged before, now fall completely flat.

In developing altruism, the main skill is to be able to recognize the humanity of the other without denying their uniqueness.

In the twenty-first century we cannot speak of responsible behavior without taking into consideration our relationship with nature.

The ethics of ancient societies was solely concerned with the relationship between humans; it was completely anthropocentric. It governed behavior within the narrow walls of a city or a village, but not outside, in the vast natural world. Nature took care of itself and, for that matter, the impact of humans on it was fairly superficial. The balance of power was in nature's favor.

With the development of science and technology, this balance was overturned—the borders between state and nature were abolished, and the manmade city, which only the day before was an enclave within nature, spread out to conquer and rule all the land.

Now, under the assault of human undertakings, nature is endangered.

Unless we hide behind environmental skepticism and tell ourselves that nothing can be certain about the evolution of the planet, it is impossible to consider the future without deep worry.

Therefore, it is essential to enlarge our ethical framework to include also the relationship between humans and the environment. Exploitation of nature reduces us to an exploiter, a thing, an instrument. There is no demeaning nature without demeaning man. The notion of responsibility must be thought of not only in terms of individual impact on the environment, which is always limited, but as members of society whose behavior affects nature in more and more significant ways.

I cannot skirt my responsibility. I cannot leave it to others on the pretext that my actions are inconsequential or that I am powerless.

Our relationship to nature must be reinvented, it cannot be solely based on rules, discipline, or customs.

In ancient India, because of the fundamental spiritualization of nature, a person's relationship to the environment was very different from ours in the twenty-first–century Western world. In Buddhism, we seldom find ideas that explicitly encourage an ecological attitude. But in the values that Buddhism defends and the excesses that it denounces, it provides a natural framework for ecological thinking.

India, unlike the Middle East, does not have myths of a great flood causing the near total destruction of humankind. In its aftermath, according to Genesis, God and Noah strike a deal: men will be subjected to God and nature to men. Then God prophesizes to Noah:

And the fear of you and the dread of you shall be upon every beast of the earth, and upon every fowl of the air, upon all that moveth upon the earth, and upon all the fishes of the sea; into your hand are they delivered.

This prophecy has indeed come true. But does God always have to be right?

There is no similar rupture in India. The earth is not reduced to a thing to be exploited, but exists in symbiosis with mankind. In the ancient Indian culture, spirits inhabit the world—genies of trees, of water, and of the earth. They often appear in Buddhist tales as protectors of the Buddha.

While the Buddha was meditating under a fig tree, a storm suddenly broke out. Muccalinda—the king of the Nagas, the genies of the waters—came out of his place and wrapped himself gently around Buddha to protect him. He encircled the Buddha seven times and opened up his hood to protect him from the torrential rain. Muccalinda did not want the Blessed One disturbed by the weather and the insects. The violent rain and wind lasted for seven days, the world was plunged into darkness. Finally the sky cleared, and the Buddha came out of his meditation. Muccalinda took the appearance of a young man and paid his respects to the Master.

Popular belief in ancient India presents numerous animistic traits, where the boundaries between humans, animals, and nature are blurry.

Animism is the belief system that probably offers the richest relationship with nature. Beyond merely finding imaginary spirits in the environment, it promotes, in its own language, an intimate contact with nature. Because animism's outlook on nature is based not on reason but on instinct and intuition, it evades our rational understanding.

The proselytizing of Muslim and evangelical missionaries in Africa and South America respectively, have caused an almost complete eradication of animist cultures. A sacred relationship with nature that existed for thousands of years is now disappearing.

Religion in the twenty-first–century places an inordinate faith in the power of science, and this leads us into further excess. Before the Enlightenment, science had to conform to religion. Now this power struggle has reversed and religion must conform to science.

Some scientists, who are ready to sacrifice the integrity of the human body on the altar of performance, think we will be replacing healthy limbs with more efficient prostheses. Perhaps these scientists cannot comprehend this "being body" or "body of presence" that dancers speak of, and which is also, to a certain extent, at the heart of yoga, tai chi, and meditation practices.

Responsibility toward nature also primordially involves the human body.

Without freeing ourselves from the *diktat* of the utilitarian, it is not possible to establish a sacred connection with nature. It can be rediscovered through traditions that are still alive, but, to certain extent, this connection must be reinvented. It is possible that the experience of presence could lead the way, insofar as it is opposed to the profane attitude that holds things within the merely temporal and utilitarian.

When they are no longer seen as sources of profit, trees, rivers, lakes, and seas have a certain presence, before which I can stand.

In *I and Thou,* Martin Buber observes while contemplating a tree:

> I can accept it as a picture: a rigid pillar in a flood of light, or splashes of green traversed by the gentleness of the blue-silver ground.
>
> I can assign it to a species and observe it as an instance, with an eye to its construction and its way of life.
>
> But it can also happen, if will and grace are joined, that as I contemplate the tree I am drawn into a relation, and the tree ceases to be an It. The power of exclusiveness has seized me.
>
> What I encounter is neither the soul of a tree nor a dryad, but the tree itself.

Buber's words here imply that the encounter with the tree is the meeting of two presences, an I and a You, not two things: an I thingi-fied with a "that."

Meditating in nature animated by this state of mind is enriching. This does not simply mean to observe the beauty of the mountains, of forests and rivers, but to place oneself in a relationship of presence. For that, one needs to abandon the point of view of a businessman, an athlete, a geographer, or a botanist who can name each plant, and to come closer to the point of view of a shaman.

During one of his numerous trips, Grotowsky went to Mexico to meet with some Indians and their shamans. One of them proposed to take him to their places of power. But Grotowski wanted to discover them by himself. He traveled the region and, little by little, found each sacred place.

Perhaps it simply requires us to not step out of ourselves, to remain receptive and open to hear what nature says deep within us, vibrat-ing like the sympathetic strings of a sitar that resonate with the main strings, resonating in another register, but in harmony with the river, the tree, or the rock. This certainly calls for great sensitivity and inner silence.

For Buddhism, the responsible person cannot be the I created by pride or confusion, which are sources of dissatisfaction. Only the self based on conventions can assure some sort of continuity. *I* stands for presence, and thus, through its interposition, presence can represent itself in the past, the future, and the present. But, as we have seen, we should not confuse presence or consciousness and its representation.

We have described compassion but not given a reason to be compas-sionate. But doesn't its value reside in the very absence of any such justification?

The deepest virtue, which is the most difficult to practice, is with-out promise of material or spiritual gain—it is virtue for no particular reason.

It is just freedom—freedom that is not without responsibility.

Acknowledgments

I T IS TO MY two main Tibetan masters that I first of all wish to express my gratitude: Geshe Rapten and Dilgo Khyentse Rinpoche, who so kindly transmitted to me a little of their knowledge.

And also to Tulku Ugyen, so skillful in revealing the nature of consciousness.

With Sayadaw U Pandita I discovered the rigor of silent retreats.

I am indebted to Joseph Goldstein for the countless pieces of advice he has given me for deepening my practice.

I also want to thank my wife Patricia for the many discussions about specific points of meditation and for her patience in reading my text again and again.

I found support in the attitude of my fellow students Steven Batchelor, Georges Dreyfus, Tom Tillemans, and Fred von Allmen, who did not sacrifice the honesty of their quest for the certainty that dogmatism offers.

I would also like to thank the translator Anna Iatsenko who has spared no effort to make the English translation understandable—not a simple matter, I should add.

And I would like to express also my gratitude to Josh Bartok, my editor at Wisdom Publications, who has supported my writing with unwavering conviction.

I remember how my master of painting, Gen Jampala, gave life to his thanka by drawing the eyes of the deity at the very end of his work.

Similarly, my friend Dean Sluyter gave life to this text: he knew how to render the clarity and lightness that I tried to give to the French version of my book. By a slow and artful work Dean has, in a way, opened the eyes of the English text. May he find here the expression of my deep gratitude.

About the Author

C HARLES GENOUD has studied and practiced Tibetan Buddhism since 1970. For a number of years, he studied with Geshe Rabten, and then continued under the guidance of Dilgo Khyentse Rinpoche. At the Institute of Buddhist Dialectics, in Dharamsala, India, he studied psychology, epistemology, and Buddhist logic. He has also practiced in the Theravadan tradition in monasteries in Burma and Thailand, and in meditation centers in Nepal, the United States, England, and France. He has taught meditation since 1995.

What to Read Next
from Wisdom Publications

Gesture of Awareness

A Radical Approach to Time, Space, and Movement

Charles Genoud

"Remarkable. Its beautiful, haiku-like teachings stretch our minds and open many new levels of understanding."—Joseph Goldstein, author of *A Heart Full of Peace* and *One Dharma: The Emerging Western Buddhism*

The World Is Made of Stories

David R. Loy

"Loy's book is like the self: layer after layer peels away, and the center is empty. But the pleasure is exactly in the exploration. At once Loy's most accessible and most philosophical work."—Alan Senauke for *Buddhadharma*

Lack & Transcendence

The Problem of Death and Life in Psychotherapy, Existentialism, and Buddhism

David R. Loy

"Brilliant. Loy plumbs the deepest and widest implications of the Buddha's 'no-self' doctrine as far as, and sometimes farther than, words can convey."—Philip Novak, author of *The World's Wisdom*

Poetry of Mindfulness, Impermanence, and Joy
John Brehm

"This collection would make a lovely gift for a poetry-loving or Dharma-practicing friend; it could also serve as a wonderful gateway to either topic for the uninitiated."—*Tricycle: The Buddhist Review*

About Wisdom Publications

Wisdom Publications is the leading publisher of classic and contemporary Buddhist books and practical works on mindfulness. To learn more about us or to explore our other books, please visit our website at wisdomexperience.org or contact us at the address below.

Wisdom Publications
199 Elm Street
Somerville, MA 02144 USA

We are a 501(c)(3) organization, and donations in support of our mission are tax deductible.

Wisdom Publications is affiliated with the Foundation for the Preservation of the Mahayana Tradition (FPMT).